What people say:

'A highly effective trainer, coach, and assessor who strives for excellence in everything she does. Her knowledge of work-based learning and adult education is outstanding and she offers good support to those she teaches and mentors, particularly through drawing on her own personal experience as an adult learner.'

Andrew Ellams, MD Ellams Associates Ltd.

'An inspirational individual and dedicated professional who gives and shares only her best. She's been very thoughtful and creative in her visionary approach to support the education sector, strengthen stakeholder relationships and guiding individuals to achieve their aspirations and goals.'

Prabhjit Kaur—PGCE(FE,) CMgr MCMI, AssocCIPD, MBA(Open) PGCE(FE).

'A detailed and passionate professional, who loves to share her knowledge with anyone who will listen.'

Joanna Kinch, MD Kinch Print Ltd.

About the Author

Rosalie Marsh is an award-winning author and a native of Lancashire with Irish roots. Today she lives in North Wales where she settled with her husband and growing family. Rosalie has written many academic, vocational, technical and research materials in her long and varied career in banking, sales management, and further education. It was during this latter period that she gained a BA (Hons) Education Degree from the Manchester Metropolitan University.

Rosalie retired to concentrate on her writing. Her first book *Just Us Two: Ned and Rosie's Gold Wing Discovery*, Winner in the 2010 International Book Awards (Travel: Recreational category), was also a UK bestseller and finalist in the USA Book News 2009 Best Books Awards. Her Lifelong Learning: Personal Effectiveness Guides build on her wide experience in the workplace along with adult and further education in the field of work-based learning.

Rosalie embraces new technologies and digital solutions. Her books therefore are always available in print and e-book formats. Rosalie writes under a pen name.

Connect with Rosalie at:
http://www.discover-rosalie.com
http://www.discover-rosalie.blogspot.com

Also by Rosalie Marsh

Just Us Two Travel Series.

Just Us Two: Ned and Rosie's Gold Wing Discovery.
Winner 2010 International Book Awards (Travel: Recreational).
Chasing Rainbows: with Just Us Two.

Lifelong Learning: Personal Effectiveness Guides.

Lifelong Learning: A View from the Coalface.
Release Your Potential: Making Sense of Personal and Professional Development.
Skills for Employability Part One: Pre-Employment.
Skills for Employability Part Two: Moving into Employment.

Future Releases.

Island Interludes: Just Us Two Escape to the Sun.
The Long Leg of Italy: Just Us Two Explore the Diversity of Italy.
Talking the Talk: Getting the Message Across.
Customer? What Customer? Some Basic Essentials in Customer Service.

Skills

for

Employability

Part Two

by
Rosalie Marsh

C
Christal Publishing

CHRISTAL PUBLISHING
11, Briarswood, Rhosrobin, WREXHAM LL11 4PX
www.christalpublishing.com

Cover Design © Christal Publishing
Images © Rosalie Marsh
www.discover-rosalie.com

First published 2012 by Christal Publishing.
ISBN 978-1-908302-20-5 Perfect Bound Soft Cover.
ISBN 978-1-908302-21-2 e-book-Kindle.
ISBN 978-1-908302-22-9 e-book-Adobe PDF.
ISBN 978-1-908302-23-6 e-book-ePub.

British Library Cataloguing in Publication Data. A catalogue record for this book is available from the British Library.

This book is printed on environmentally friendly paper from responsible sources.

Contents

Foreword

The target audience for this book is diverse. This includes those at pre-employment stage e.g. school leavers up to graduates; 16-18 year old unemployed who have not obtained sufficient grades to follow their preferred path; returners to work; those with disabilities who are seeking a change of employment; those in employment and seeking to enhance their prospects or are between jobs. Currently [01.2012], there are over 1 million people in the UK who are classed as 'Not in Employment, Education, or Training' (NEETS).

Many do not have the life skills and/or a basic understanding of what is required to become and stay employed and enhance their future. This book—Part Two of *Skills for Employability*—will provide essential information to fill the gaps identified through research, enhance the prospects of a successful interview, and impress employers.

There are many publications, which address the gaps in adult literacy, numeracy, and Key Stage 4. The whole raft of knowledge needed for employability and personal development—on which business success depends—is not currently fully represented. This book will address those aspects of employability relating to business and work-related practice. Currently, most practitioners engaged in work-based learning, design, and develop their own training programmes. This book will reduce the burden. It is designed to be a non-threatening user-friendly resource for anyone to use whether or not they attend a formal training course.

Those seeking and moving into employment may be familiar with much of what is normally (but often not) contained in an induction programme. This book will enhance the process; learners will be entering employment forearmed; it will be a reference in the future. Much of the content is embedded as compulsory requirements in the mandatory units of various vocational qualifications.

The chapters are signposted to units accredited in the Qualifications and Credit Framework (QCF) including SSA Units 14.1 Foundations for Learning and Life and 14.2 Preparation for Work; OCR Personal Life Skills; OCR Employability Skills; City and Guilds Employability and Personal Development (7546) Units. The knowledge in this book could be presented for accreditation of prior learning and therefore speed up achievement for the learner.

Author Note:
'Essential Skills Wales (ESW) are the fundamental qualifications for reading, writing, maths and IT in Wales. They're designed to help you apply your skills to real situations—from adding up bills to creating a CV. You can get a qualification in three skill areas—Communication, Application of Number and Information and Communication Technology (ICT).'

http://www.cityandguilds.com/57650.html?s=1 03.02.2012

'In Wales, the accreditation end date for Wider Key Skills has been extended to August 2014. The Wider Key Skills standards are currently being revised and it is anticipated that the revised qualifications will become part of the Essential Skills Wales suite from September 2012.'

http://www.ocr.org.uk/qualifications/type/esw/ 03.02.2012.

Therefore, in the interests of inclusiveness, the topics are signposted—where relevant—to Functional Skills, Essential Skills Wales (Communication, Application of Number, Information Communication Technology [ICT]); and the Wider Key Skills Working with Others, Improving Own Learning and Performance, and Problem Solving.

Features and Benefits

Features and benefits for those seeking and moving into employment:

Features.

➢ Each chapter/section will detail the learning outcomes and relevance to other qualifications.

➢ At the end of each topic there will be a series of questions/activities for self-assessment to check learner progress. In turn, this will add to a sense of achievement.

➢ Learners will be able to measure how far they have travelled.

➢ Much of the content will feed into and is signposted to Functional Skills; the Awards and Certificates in Employability and Personal Development; and/or Personal Life and Employability Skills, all of which are linked to the Qualifications and Credit Framework (QCF).

➢ All content will relate to the current gaps in knowledge & understanding and softer skills for those who are pre-employment, e.g. Year 10 and Year-11 school leavers; 16-18 year old unemployed; returners to work; learners with disabilities who are seeking a change of employment, are in employment and seeking to enhance their prospects or are between jobs.

➢ The book will have some illustrations to enhance text.

> There are links to websites, e.g., for legislation and further current information. This will provide more interaction and variety for the learner and ensure currency of information.

Adult Literacy and Numeracy will not be addressed in this book, as there are many excellent resources available.

Benefits.

After completing *Skills for Employability Part Two: Moving into Employment*, learners will:

> Have more awareness of the standards of behaviour and requirements of employers.

> Be introduced to health and safety in the workplace and have an awareness of employment rights and responsibilities (both employer and employee).

> Have completed short practical activities that aim to test their understanding.

> Have raised their self-esteem and confidence.

> Have an awareness and understanding of the business environment.

> Have an awareness of good customer service.

> Have some basic knowledge and understanding, which will feed into the Awards/Certificates in Employability and Personal Life Skills/Development, vocational qualifications, or company training programmes.

Features and benefits for teachers, tutors, and trainers:

Feature.
Available in print and e-book formats for most readers.

Benefit.

Time and cost savings. A ready-made resource reduces time and cost of design and/or photocopying.

Feature.
In print form, *Skills for Employability Part Two* can be used in the traditional way with everyone having their own copy.

Benefits.

It can be taken away by the learner to be absorbed as part of homework or an assignment.

It can be issued as a resource for the course to be used as intended—as a workbook.

Feature.
Available in a variety of e-book formats worldwide:

➢ Kindle and Kindle Apps for desktop, iBook, Android etc.

➢ Adobe Digital Editions PDF for desktop and readers, available for download from e-retailers worldwide.

➢ ePub. Apple iBookstore, Sony eBooks, B&N Nook, Diesel eBooks, Kobo, B&T Blio, Smashwords.com and other e-retailers.

Benefits.

➢ Can be downloaded to a PC and be tutor led via presentation screen or whiteboard with learners following from the print version.

➢ Can be downloaded to college computers or a hand-held reader for full interaction with tutors and learners.

- ➢ Cost effective. Budget will go further.
- ➢ Learners can adjust the font size and background colour to suit individual sight preferences, thus overcoming one of the barriers to reading enjoyment.
- ➢ The majority of learners are used to technology and reading on-screen.
- ➢ User-friendly.

Overview of
Skills for Employability Part Two

Well Done! By opening this book, you have taken the first step to increasing your skills and knowledge to develop yourself, make you more employable, and enhance your future.

You may be on the verge of leaving school and looking for employment. You may have completed a course of study following leaving school or not worked at all. On the other hand, you may be in employment and are looking to better yourself and achieve those goals that you have only previously dreamed of achieving. The aim of this book is to fill any gaps in skills or knowledge and understanding you may have which prevent you from gaining employment or progressing in your current or future employment. It will prepare you for the world of work beyond your present horizons and set you on the road to achieve your full potential.

As already explained, the topics relate closely to other learning programmes. Learning here is flexible and completed in bite-size chunks where you can build 'stepping stones' to the future. Depending on 'where you are at' you can take as little or as much as you need from the learning experience.

The topics in this book also relate very closely to some of those skills that are an essential part of being employable. These are called Functional Skills.

What are Functional Skills?

Functional Skills describe different areas of skills and knowledge, which underpin effective performance in everyday life, both work and leisure. They are needed for continued employability and prosperity. They are a means of proving that you are working at the level needed in key areas of competence for your job role, and have often been underdeveloped and unrecognised in the past. Tasks you complete in one functional skill area often provide evidence for another.

'Functional Skills are the fundamental applied skills in English, Information and Communication Technology (ICT) and Mathematics—or Number—that help people to gain the most from life, learning and work. The skills are learning tools that enable people: to apply their knowledge and understanding to everyday life, to engage competently and confidently with others, to solve problems in both familiar and unfamiliar situations, to develop personally and professionally as positive citizens who can actively contribute to society.'
(Source Ofqual /09/4558)

To put it a little clearer, you need to be able to read and understand instructions and information, write clearly and spell correctly so that others understand you, and to be able to speak clearly and take part in conversations and discussions with people you work with.

You need to know how to handle numbers in everyday situations such as shopping, working out your wages to make sure you have been paid correctly, working out how much you will need to fill your car with petrol etc. So by mathematics, (do not freeze and hold up your hands in horror when you hear the word!) we really mean using numbers in all sorts of everyday situations at work, at home and in leisure.

Most organisations use computers—we are in a technological age. You will probably have used computers in school. If you have a computer at home, you will possibly have been able to widen your skills. However, there are still many homes without a computer or it is used mainly for surfing the Internet and playing games. It may be that your parents control the computer and you have not been allowed to use the various software packages such as Microsoft® Word or Microsoft® Works for letters and CV's, or simple spreadsheets for planning your budget or holiday.

You may have a job where you just use the system and are not involved in actually putting information onto the system. That is OK but you do need to be familiar with a computer and the keyboard and be competent at a basic level if you are going to increase your employability. If you work in an office *of any kind,* you will need good ICT skills. This was covered in *Skills for Employability Part One: Pre-Employment.*

So working with other people; dealing with customers; improving your skills and standard of working; being able to work through and solve the kind of problems which crop up; are all achieved by having good levels of English, Mathematics (number), and computer skills. They underpin everything. Your employer, training provider and/or local college should have more information on these and the awards and certificates mentioned earlier.

NB. *'Functional Skills are available in England and Northern Ireland. Wales has its own policy and has developed Essential Skills Wales.'*
http://wales.gov.uk/topics/educationandskills/learningproviders/
essentialskillswales/

Skills for Employability Part Two: Moving into Employment is made up of chapters, which cover a number of topics.

Employment Rights and Responsibilities (ERR) covers: your rights and responsibilities as an employee, your employers rights and responsibilities, an introduction to health and safety in the workplace, security, confidentiality, a self assessment checklist, 'What do I need to do better / learn?', check your knowledge and signposting to QCF units.

Managing your Money covers: understanding your pay slip, tax and insurance, budgeting your money, income, and outgoings, check your knowledge and signposting to QCF units.

The Business Environment covers: what employers expect, working effectively in the workplace,.check your knowledge and signposting to QCF units.

The Importance of Good Customer Service covers: 'Who is my customer?', internal and external customers, dealing with customer problems, improving customer service, check your knowledge and signposting to QCF units.

Healthy Living covers: eating well, exercise, sleep, personal hygiene, check your knowledge and signposting to QCF Units.

Progression. 'Where do I go from here?' points you to the next stage of your journey.

Each chapter will detail the learning outcome (tell you what you will be learning). There will be a series of tasks for you to complete along the way as well as some links to the Internet where you can explore the topics in more detail. This is to give you some variety in your learning journey and to check your progress. In turn, you will have a sense of achievement and will be able to see how far you have travelled.

At the end of each chapter, there will be signposting to the Personal Life, Development/Employability Awards and Certificates, and/or Functional Skills. Therefore, if you read the topics carefully and complete all the tasks you could have some evidence to go towards this. This is called Accreditation of Prior Learning. No learning is ever wasted; learning can come from all sorts of situations both formal and informal, from work or from leisure activities. Once you have learned something, there is no need to go through the process again if it appears in a different qualification. Although this book is not designed to give you a qualification in itself—more to help you develop yourself—the bite-sized chunks mentioned in the Personal Life/Development and Employability Skills qualifications are given a credit value and are transferable. This book will contribute to the knowledge and understanding needed whether or not you are undertaking the qualification at this time.

Please turn now to Chapter One and continue your journey.

Chapter One.Employment Rights and Responsibilities (ERR)

In this chapter we will start the ball rolling with a short re-cap on the basic health and safety topics covered in Part One before looking at what we mean by *Employment* Rights and Responsibilities (ERR).

'Surely', you are saying to yourself, 'you mean *my* rights as an employee and my employer's responsibilities to *me* as an employee?' Sorry to disillusion you but employers have rights as well, and *you* as an employee, have responsibilities. You have a 'duty of care' to yourself and those near to you.

Think on that for a moment!

This may be a change of mindset for you. It is however, crucial that you understand this if you want to keep in a job and move on to a better life.

In *Skills for Employability Part One: Pre-Employment,* we looked at health and safety when using ICT. You may not have read this but if you have, a re-cap on health and safety is never too much. Therefore, we will revisit this and expand on it as we look at yours and your employer's employment rights and responsibilities.

These include:

> ➢ Employment rights.
> ➢ Responsibilities for health and safety in the workplace.
> ➢ Responsibilities for security in the workplace.
> ➢ Equal Opportunities.
> ➢ Codes of Practice and ethical standards.
> ➢ Data protection and confidentiality.

Employment Rights.

When you saw the advertisement for the job, it would probably have stated what the main terms of the job were. It may have said what the basic duties were and what skills you needed. Very often things like the number of holidays are stated.

This should have been discussed in more depth at your interview where you would have had the opportunity to ask about anything that you were not sure of. When an offer of a job was made, the letter (especially in a large organisation) may have set out some terms and conditions of employment. You may have only been given the terms verbally and told when to start. This is quite common in smaller firms.

Contract of Employment.

> 'An employment contract, or contract of employment, is an agreement between an employer and an employee which sets out their employment rights, responsibilities, and duties. These are called the 'terms' of the contract.'
>
> http://www.direct.gov.uk/en/Employment/Employees/EmploymentContractsAnd Conditions/DG_10027905 (sourced 29.05.2012)

This contract or agreement does not have to be in writing. However, you are entitled to have the main terms of the job in writing within two months of starting work. Accepting the job constitutes a contract. Starting work shows that have accepted the terms of the employment.

The law surrounding contracts of employment is very detailed and I won't attempt to discuss every point here. I will just outline the main points. Many organisations have a Quality Manual or Employee Handbook of some kind, which details, according to law, what you are entitled to as part of your employment. These are known as your statutory rights. Some organisations go over and above what is required in law and offer more.

Some points that should be in your contract are:

Your name and that of your employer and the start date of the job.

Job title and location of work.

The date when continuous employment started. Sometimes you may move to another post in the same organisation and knowing if your previous employment length of service counts towards continuous employment is very, very important as it could affect redundancy payments, unfair dismissal, or even holiday entitlement.

Duties involved— a brief description.

A fixed term contract should state the period of time the contract is for.

Details of rates of pay and it if will increase after a certain period. You may be on a national minimum wage and this should be stated along with the rate of pay. Currently (Oct 2011), someone of 21 years of age or over should receive £6.08 per hour. There are lower rates for 16-17 years and 18-20 years. The apprentice rate for someone under 19 or 19 and over in the first year of an apprenticeship is different again. If you are of compulsory school age, there is no statutory entitlement and employment rights may be different. For current information, check out:

http://www.direct.gov.uk/en/Employment/Employees/The NationalMinimumWage/DG_10027201

You may be working under an agency contract, which is quite common nowadays as some organisations have a core group of workers and hire extra if the level of work demands it.

Full details of hours of work, holidays (paid or unpaid). If there is what is called a collective agreement. That is when an agreement has been reached with, for instance, a trade union or staff association. If so, your contract should state who can negotiate on your behalf and which ones apply to you. The agreement applies to you even if you are not a member of the trade union or staff association.

Bank holiday and public holiday arrangements. Contrary to popular opinion, bank holidays are not an entitlement. Bank holidays are when banks are closed, as well as some other businesses. Most employers recognise bank and public holidays in some way and if you cannot take a holiday will give days off in lieu or extra pay. Your contract should state if you get a bank holiday or public holiday or both. If you work through an agency it is crucial that you check this and not assume anything, as employees in the same organisation that you are contracted to work in as an agency worker can have different arrangements or 'terms of contract'. *Your* contract would be with the agency.

Holiday arrangements. The bank and public holidays may be included in your entitlement. This is quite common. Your basic entitlement if you work five days a week is 28 days or 5.6 weeks. Your contract may state that your entitlement includes bank and public holidays or if your entitlement is plus bank and public holidays. If you work part time, your entitlement will be worked out on what we call pro rata. It is actually important to be clear whether your pro rata entitlement is worked out minus bank and public holidays or including them. Your contract should state what the arrangements of pay or time off in lieu are, if any, if you work on a bank or public holiday.

Sick leave arrangements and pay.

Notice for termination of employment—on both sides, if the job is permanent or temporary.

Details of grievance and disciplinary procedures.

Pension arrangements should be stated. Many organisations have a company pension scheme to which the employee can contribute. Others do not, leaving the employee to make their own provision for a private pension over and above the state pension.

**New rules come into effect from October 2012 whereby all employers—starting with larger companies—must auto enrol eligible employees into a workplace pension scheme if they are not already in a qualifying scheme. Depending on the number of employees, these new arrangements will take place between October 2012 and 2016.

Briefly, employees must be:

> ➢ Aged 22 or over.
> ➢ Not already in a qualifying workplace pension.
> ➢ Under state pension age.
> ➢ Earn more than a minimum amount a year (currently £8,105—figure may change each April).
> ➢ Work or usually work in the UK.

http://www.thepensionsregulator.gov.uk/workplacepensions.html will have the most recent information.

The purpose of making pension schemes compulsory is to ensure that you have an adequate income when you retire.

This list of what should be included in your contact of employment is not exhaustive. Employment law is very detailed and changes over time. Take a look at these excellent government websites for current details:

http://www.direct.gov.uk/en/Employment/Employees/index.htm

http://www.bis.gov.uk/search?keywords=contracts+of+employment&type=all

Pay and Pay Slips.

An employee, with a few rare exceptions, has the right to know when and how they will be paid. Details are normally contained in the contract of employment. But what if you haven't been given one yet? You need to know from day one how you will be paid and how much. You also need to know when you will be paid, e.g., Thursday? Friday? A certain day each month? It is your money. You have worked hard for it. You are entitled to know.

Your pay slip must detail the gross amount of your wages (before any deductions).

> ➤ You may pay a trade union or pay into a medical insurance. This is a fixed deduction and should be listed.
> ➤ The individual amount of any variable deductions e.g. Income Tax and National Insurance.
> ➤ The net amount (after deductions) of your wages
> ➤ If you wage is paid part cash and part into the bank for instance, this must be stated clearly.

A pay slip is not required to have, but usually does have, your National Insurance number, Income Tax code, pay rate including overtime rates, and any bonus.

Weekly pay.
If you are paid on a weekly basis, you may be paid what is known as 'a week in hand'. This means that what you worked one week will be paid out the next. You may have to complete a time sheet or a clock card so that the wages department can work out how much you will be paid. (*For instance, you may have worked some overtime or had some unpaid leave.*) This is normally done at the start of the following week and the money either paid into the bank by the end of the week— in which case you would just receive a pay slip; be paid by cheque along with a pay slip—not very common now; or be paid in cash in a pay packet along with the pay slip.

One point to remember is that if you are paid a week in hand, you will in effect, feel that you have worked a week for nothing. This is hard if you have been out of work and you must take this into account when working out how you will manage.

Monthly Pay.
If you are what is known as 'salaried staff', you will receive your pay once a month. As your salary will be an annual one, it is easy for the wages department to work out your pay.

Usually any overtime worked is paid in arrears. Your organisation will have details of when the cut-off date is for working this out and paying it that month. They normally do the salaries early in the month so that all the details can go to the bank for payment by a certain date. Some organisations pay on the 21st of the month. Some pay on the 15th and some right at the end of the month. In any case, the basic salary is normally paid for that month. For instance, if they pay out on the 21st, they usually pay for the whole month along with any overtime or expenses claimed for the previous month.

If you are moving from a weekly paid job to a monthly paid role, this can cause budgeting problems. For instance, you would have your last week's pay from your previous job (a week in hand) but there would probably be a gap before you were paid in your new job. The leap from weekly to monthly usually means that you have got a better job so it is worth it in the end. It is something to consider though.

Income Tax and National Insurance.
In Chapter Two. Managing Your Money, we look in detail at how your pay is worked out and what deductions are taken out before you even see your pay.

Working Time Regulations.

The Working Time Regulations are not an employment regulation as many think they are. They are actually a health and safety regulation. They have been put in place to ensure that you do not pose a risk to your own health and safety, and that of others, by working for too long without an adequate break.

Usually you can only work a maximum of 48 hours a week, averaged out over 17 weeks.

There are, however certain jobs which do not come into this regulation.

You also have the right to opt out of working under the 48-hour week limits. This must be in writing and must be your choice. You cannot be forced into opting out.

<u>The working week.</u>

Apart from the normal day-to-day duties that you carry out, other aspects of the job count as 'work'. For instance:

> Any job-related training, on the premises or somewhere else.
> If you travel as part of your work, job-related travelling time is counted, e.g., a sales rep.
> A business lunch. Many deals are completed away from the office, so working lunches are counted.
> Overtime both paid and unpaid. Yes, strange as it may seem, some of us do work a lot of unpaid overtime.
> If you are on call, time spent on-call at the workplace.

<u>Do I get paid for breaks at work?</u>

That depends on your employer, and what is in your contract of employment; or what is usual practice in the organisation. There are tea breaks, lunch breaks and other short breaks.

Do you smoke? Do you need to nip out to smoke a cigarette during your shift or outside your break? For non-smokers, this can be a bone of contention. After all, they are busy beavering away while you are having an un-scheduled break. If you like a cigarette, try to keep to normal rest breaks.

<u>How long, and when, can I take a break?</u>

> If you are an adult over 18 years old, you must be given a twenty-minute break if you are being asked to work over six hours. You cannot save the time up and finish work early. A coffee break or lunch break can count as your rest break. Any extra breaks are at the discretion of your employer.

- ➢ You cannot split it into shorter snatched breaks. You must take the 20 minutes in one block. You *can* go off the premises.
- ➢ Some organisations have strict security procedures and often it is easier to stay in the canteen or rest room.
- ➢ You, as an employee have the right to a break as mentioned above. For your own well-being and efficiency, you should take them.
- ➢ Rest breaks are normally timed to the benefit of the business needs and your employer has the right to decide when you take your break.

I did say earlier that your employer has rights as well as you didn't I? Just one example. The needs of the business come first!

Breaks between one working day and the next one.

The regulations states that you should have a clear eleven hours break between ending one working day and starting the next.

Breaks between one working week and the next.

You should have a clear, uninterrupted twenty-four hours a week.

You should have a clear, uninterrupted 48 hours a fortnight.

Exceptions.

Some jobs are exempt from the Working Time Regulations.

Regulations are often updated. Go to:

http://www.direct.gov.uk/en/Employment/Employees/WorkingHoursAndTimeOff/index.htm

Flexible Working.

Many jobs are now based around working from home. You may have a job where you work between home and the office.

Your rights depend on your legal status i.e. are you employed, self-employed or a home worker?

Requesting flexible working arrangements.

You can ask for flexible working arrangements under various circumstances.

Providing that you are an employee, (not agency worker or in the armed forces), have completed 26 weeks continuous service and have not made another application in the past 12 months, you have the statutory right to apply under certain conditions. For example:

> You have or expect to have a parental responsibility for a child under 17 years. (Under 18 years if disabled and receives Disability Living Allowance-DLA).
> You have certain caring responsibilities.

Although you have the right to make an application, your employer has the right to assess it on business grounds.

If you do not have a legal right to request flexible working, nothing is stopping you from requesting anyway. Sometimes flexible working can work to the mutual advantage of both you and your employer.

Rights as a parent.

There are many regulations and arrangements surrounding pregnancy, maternity rights, paternal rights, and adoption right in the workplace.

Go to http://www.direct.gov.uk/en/Employment/index.htm and follow the links where there is up-to-date information on all these topics, including maternity leave and pay.

Check Point!
Name three things that should be in your contract of
employment.

1.

2.

3.

How long can you work without a break?

What is the National Minimum Rate of pay for someone aged
19 years and who is not an apprentice?

Now go back and check your knowledge?

Have you taken time to follow the Internet links?

Responsibilities for health and safety in the workplace.

The workplace today is a much safer place than in days gone by. Many things, which we take for granted, have been put there in law to ensure our safety and well-being.

Some of the things we are required to do are enshrined in various types of law such as Acts of Parliament, Regulations, Approved Codes of Practice (ACOPs) Statutory Codes of Practice (SCOPs) and Guidance Notes.

As we want to keep this to the general things you need to be aware of, we are not going to go too deep into all of these. There are many publications about and the Internet is a huge source of information, as you will find out from the links that I will give you along the way.

One major Act of Parliament is the Health and Safety at Work Act 1974 (HASWA). The Factories Act 1961 is another under which it is an offence to remove a guard from a machine. I remember years ago when this regulation came in, all the cotton mills, for example, had to have guards made and fitted around the machines. This provided a lot of work for the engineering firms in the area (which was lost when the mills closed down).

The Offices, Shops and Railway Premises Act 1963 (OSRP) applies, as the name implies, to other types of working environments.

Health and Safety at Work Act etc 1974 (HASWA).

This Act applies to every workplace. Every workplace is required to display the official poster, which lays out the responsibilities of your employer to you, and you to your employer. Everyone who steps foot on the premises is covered by the Act. Under the Act, they also have responsibilities whilst on the premises.

The 'health' part of the Act covers general risks as well as mental health, stress, drugs, alcohol, and smoking.

The 'safety' part of the 1974 Act brought together existing industrial laws.

The 'at work' part of the Act means when you are working in any situation or location. This also means someone who travels about in a company car as part of his or her work.

The 'etc.' part of the Act is often forgotten. How often do you see those three letters? HASWA is an enabling Act, which means that regulations can be added without having to go back to parliament. The six European Community Directives became regulations in the UK under the Act in 1992. They are known as the six-pack. More on that later.

Employees have a duty of care to **themselves and others.** They must take 'reasonable care of their own health, safety, and welfare at work, and that of others who may be affected by their acts or omissions'. Section 7(a) HASWA 1974.

Under Section 7(b), employees have a **duty to their employers.** All employees must 'co-operate with their employer in all things which he does in order to discharge his health and safety responsibilities'. Employees have to obey the organisation's health and safety policy, wear the personal protective equipment provided, and respond to an evacuation signal.

Larking around in work happens. This however, can be dangerous if under **Section 8** you 'intentionally or recklessly interfere with or misuse anything provided in the interest of health, safety, and welfare'. Wedging open fire doors with a fire extinguisher is an offence under the Act.

Employers have a duty under Section 2(1) 'to ensure, as far as is reasonably practicable, the health, safety and welfare at work of all his/her employees'.

(Health and Safety. Morris. 1997 p8-10)

I am not going to go into all the sections of the Act here. I just want to highlight that *both* the employer *and* the employee have rights and responsibilities.

The Health and Safety Executive (HSE) is responsible for enforcing health and safety at work. Your employer may receive a visit from the health and safety inspector at some point.

Health, Safety and Security Regulations in the Workplace.

As I have just said, everyone has a duty of care to others.

'In addition, the Health and Safety at Work Act 1974 requires employers and employees to take reasonable care for the health and safety of everyone at work, including visitors and other non-employees who use the premises.'

(Source:.http://www.worksmart.org.uk/rights/i_have_heard_about_a_duty_of 07.03.2012)

I said earlier that the HASWA was an enabling act, which allowed other regulations to be added to it without going back to Parliament.

Six European Union Directives (known as the six-pack) came into force on January 1st 1993 and were embedded in the Health and Safety at Work Act 1974 as Regulations:

> ➢ Display Screen Equipment Regulations 1992 (amended 2002).
> ➢ Manual Handling Operations 1992.
> ➢ Workplace (Health, Safety, and Welfare) Regulations 1992.
> ➢ Provision and Use of Work Equipment Regulations 1992 (amended 1998).
> ➢ Personal Protective Equipment at Work Regulations 1992.
> ➢ The Management of Health and Safety at Work Regulations 1992—(more commonly known as the Management Regulations).

Therefore, your employer must make sure that:

> There are safe entry and exit routes.
> There is a safe working environment.
> There are reasonable welfare facilities.
> Equipment is maintained in good working order and kept in a safe condition.
> Articles and substances are transported safely.
> They provide protective clothing where needed.
> They give you information on health and safety (the HSE poster should be displayed where all can see it easily).
> You are given instruction where needed.
> You are given training in your role.
> You have adequate supervision when needed.

You have the right to be protected when using machinery of any kind and an organisation must comply with the law in making sure that all equipment including electrical equipment is safe. This includes computers.

However, you *also* have responsibilities as an employee and must not do anything, which could endanger yourself or others.

You may not be in an office as such but work or go into an office attached to the shop or production floor. The next section of this chapter deals with that and some basic 'good housekeeping'.

The workstation or desk.

> Make sure that the wires are not a tangled mess. It is easy to have a heavy cable resting on a much lighter one but this can cause something to disconnect. Try to have all the cables free from each other. Do not wrap them over each other as this can break the finer wires inside.
> Slips, trips, and falls are the biggest cause of time off work. Make sure that there are no trailing wires for other people to trip over. Keep wires away from main traffic areas. If that is impossible,

they should be taped down or enclosed in a special cover.
- ➤ Take regular breaks away from the screen if your work involves mainly computer work. This could be planned into your schedule as part of the day's work.
- ➤ Adjust your screen. There should be an eye distance of 50cm-90cm.
- ➤ Adjust your seat to the right height for you so that you are not straining with a viewing angle of about 20°. Adjust the backrest.

Task:

Take a look at the website below for more details on how to avoid strain and what kind of chair you should be using. Your chair is actually a work tool.

http://www.healthandsafety.co.uk/CHOOSING%20THE%2 0RIGHT%20CHAIR.pdf

- ➤ Do not have drinks near the keyboard or your work. A simple accident can cause the loss of information on the PC, or on paper-based copies of the information. This can be expensive.
- ➤ Clear all rubbish from the desk into the waste bin.
- ➤ Make sure that the desk, computer, printer, and other equipment are kept clean.

A dirty screen means that you have to strain to see properly. A dirty keyboard and computer means that dust can get inside and could cause a malfunction. Apart from anything else, it doesn't give a good impression to either other people you work with or visitors. If you take care of your working environment, customers and colleagues can see that you will take care of them and your work. The office of a small works e.g. an engineering works, by its location in a partitioned area off the shop floor soon gets dusty. Do not be shy of picking up a cloth and dusting the screen, desk, and computer. You will be showing that you care and have standards, which will reflect on your work.

You should always follow manufacturer's instructions for cleaning and maintenance.

More information at http://www.hse.gov.uk *and*

http://www.pcs.org.uk/en/resources/health_and_safety/he alth_and_safety_legal_summaries/display_screen_equipm ent_regulations.cfm

Task:

If you are already in employment, look around you. What do you see? Is everything clean and tidy? Think about the points above. Could anything be improved?

Make a note.

Can you put things right? If so—do so.

If you are not in employment, and have a computer at home, look and see what you could improve on. Are things piled up in a mess? Are there half-drunk cups of tea or coffee lying around on job applications and CV's etc.?

Food for thought! A tidy space means more space.

The Workplace (Health, Safety and Welfare) Regulations 1992.

These regulations provide more information and detail about what is required.

The main requirements of these regulations cover:

Work environment. There should be effective ventilation, a reasonable temperature, adequate lighting plus emergency lighting, sufficient space to work, suitable workstations, (this does not always mean a computer workstation). If the workstation is outside the building there must be protection from adverse weather conditions.

Safety. This means that there must be designated traffic routes e.g. in a factory or engineering workshop or warehouse, which pedestrians and vehicles, e.g. forklift truck, can use to move around safely. Floors, doors, gates, and escalators must be properly constructed and maintained. Windows and skylights must be safe. If there is a danger from falling objects from above, safeguards must be put in place. Hazard warning signs must be provided.

Facilities. Sufficient toilets, washing facilities, and an adequate supply of safe drinking water. If the water from a tap is not safe, there are special labels to warn you that *'this water is not safe to drink'*. There must be adequate seating. See above for seating at a computer but there are other situations where seating is needed or should be made available. Facilities include somewhere to hang your clothing. (Many organisations just have a coat rack. Some provide lockers.) Adequate rest areas and facilities for people who eat at work are covered under these Regulations.

The Control of Substances Hazardous to Health 1999 (COSHH).

All hazardous substances (such as toxic cleaning substances) must be stored in a special environment and users provided with protective clothing free of charge. This also applies to the kitchen/canteen area where cleaning materials should be labelled properly and kept out of reach in their own containers, in their own cupboard. Labels must be clear. Do not be tempted to decant them into another container with a different label, or even worse, unlabelled. The consequences of them being drunk or ingested do not bear thinking about.

You would need rubber gloves when dealing with bleach and other strong cleaning materials. In a workshop, solvents for cleaning, paint and thinners should be kept in a fireproof cupboard with only authorised people allowed to use them. Of course, personal protective equipment comes in here, as gloves should be worn. If there is a strong smell or fumes, then a mask should be worn.

In many jobs, the last one in has the canteen duties so this does apply to all sorts of people and jobs. In any case, even if you are in a position of responsibility, you need to know about these regulations so that you can make sure that your staff complies with them.

Your employer is responsible for carrying out a COSHH assessment on any substances, which could cause harm. No one is exempt. No matter how small the workforce or even if you are self-employed, the assessment must be carried out.

I am just looking at a bottle of correction fluid. It is quite a small bottle. This is not dangerous. Is it? If you have one handy, look at the hazard warnings on the bottle. They will shock you.

What do you see? I can see a symbol which means highly inflammable, a symbol which means it is an irritant (could cause damage if inhaled), and a symbol which means that it is dangerous to the environment. I also have the same correction fluid in the form of a tape, which is on an enclosed roll. It is called a Pocket Mouse. There are no warning signs— a much better option.

More at: http://www.hse.gov.uk/chip/phrases.htm

Personal Protective Equipment at Work Regulations 1992 (PPE). Protective clothing and equipment must be provided when risks cannot be eliminated. This must be free of charge, fit properly and be maintained in good condition. Under the Noise at Work Regulations 1989, this includes ear defenders where noise is a hazard. Bar staff in a pub or restaurant are usually provided with an apron or a special uniform. Your employer will have determined what PPE is required when the Risk Assessment was carried out.

Provision and Use of Work Equipment Regulations 1992 (PUWER). This is wide-ranging and covers all equipment. If you work in an engineering works or factory of any kind, you will naturally expect that equipment will be well maintained and be told how to use it. Not so obvious is the equipment in an office environment of any kind. These regulations also apply to photocopiers and fax machines. All equipment must be well maintained. You should have appropriate training and instruction on how to use the equipment.

Manual Handling Operations Regulations 1992 relate to lifting and handling items and equipment of any kind. You might be asked to bring in some parcels. Are they heavy? Do you deal with stationery items in an office? That is not so obvious is it?

Automated or mechanised equipment should be used if possible or appropriate but if you have to move items you should be trained properly how to bend and lift to minimise injury. You should use a trolley of some sort for transporting heavier or bulky items. You may find that you are given instruction in this during your induction. It depends on the job. In retail, distribution, or delivery, a sack trolley is often used. In some jobs a forklift truck is often used which moves down the designated traffic areas. *(These must only be operated by someone who has completed an approved forklift training course.)* Warning signs should be around to warn pedestrians of the danger if they get in the way.

Reporting of Injuries, Diseases, and Dangerous Occurrences Regulations 1995 (RIDDOR).

Serious workplace accidents, occupational diseases and a dangerous occurrence or what is known as a 'near miss' (a slip, trip or fall that could have resulted in injury), must be reported.

'I am not hurt, it is just a little bruise', you may think to yourself. But when you reached out to save yourself (after tripping over that strap from a messenger/computer bag which has been carelessly left trailing in the gangway, or slipping on the plastic covering left lying around on the floor), you didn't realise it at the time but you banged your leg, or you pulled a muscle. You may have to have time off work. Worse still, next time someone could bang their head on the filing cabinet drawer, which has been left open after use. They could break their neck when they try to save themselves when they fall.

The exact incident must be recorded so that there is 1) a record in case of further problems and 2) so that the hazards can be removed and further injury be avoided.

If someone has a hospital stay of over three days, special forms are used to report it to the Health and Safety Executive (HSE).

First Aid.

Every organisation must have adequate first aid provision.

Your employer must ensure than anyone who is injured receives immediate attention. Failure to do so could result in death. The regulations apply to all premises—even those with fewer than five employees.

The First Aid Kit must be easily accessible. There should be a notice saying where it is, who the appointed First Aider or Appointed Person is, together with their contact details, e.g., mobile or telelephone number(and telephone extension if applicable).

The size of the First Aid Kit depends on the numbers in the organisation. They are usually green with a white cross and it will say for how many people it is sufficient. If items are used, they must be replaced.

Fire.

There are legal requirements for fire precautions and fire safety. Briefly, there should be sufficient fire extinguishers of the right type placed where they can be easily reached. The area around them should be kept clear. They must not be removed other than to control a fire. They must be checked and maintained on a regular basis by approved organisations.

There should be a notice advising all persons where the fire exits are and where the meeting point outside is.

All exits point to an escape route must have a sign saying 'FIRE EXIT'. In the event of a fire, do not use a lift.

Evacuation procedures must be followed. Your organisation should take you through these during your induction, along with other essential health and safety information. If you are lucky, you will be sent on a basic health and safety course.

Before 1997, all fire extinguishers used to be made in different colours containing different materials for different sorts of fire. Now they are all red (unless there are some of the old ones, which have not reached the end of their life and have not been changed) with a label to say what it contains and what class of fire it is for. By class, we mean type but they are all grouped into Class A, B, C, D, E, and F as follows:

> ➤ Class A is for SOLIDS (paper, wood, plastic etc.)
> ➤ Class B is for FLAMMABLE LIQUIDS (paraffin, petrol, oil etc.)
> ➤ Class C is for FLAMMABLE GASES (propane, butane, methane etc.)
> ➤ Class D is for METALS (aluminium, magnesium, titanium etc.)
> ➤ Class E is for fires involving ELECTRICAL APPARATUS
> ➤ Class F is for COOKING OIL & FAT etc.

The colour coding is as follows:

> ➤ Water—Red—suitable for Class A fires.
> ➤ Foam–Cream—for Class A & B fires.
> ➤ Dry Powder—Blue—for Class A, B, & C. It is Multi-purpose.
> ➤ Carbon Dioxide (CO2)—Black—for electrical fires.

There is a 'wet chemical' extinguisher for Class F fires and a special one or metal fires.

Now that fire extinguishers are all red, there can be a coloured label to indicate what type it is using the colour coding above.

Task:

That was a big section. You don't have to know all the regulations in detail, but you do have to be aware of the main points so that you keep healthy and safe.

Take a break and then answer the following to check your understanding.

To whom do you report health and safety matters?

a) Supervisor.

b) Manager.

c) Friend.

d) Health and safety officer.

Answer:

Why do you have to report accidents and 'near misses'?

What would you do if you found a door propped up with a fire extinguisher?

Which fire extinguisher would you use for electrical fires?

Risks.

You have a right to work in a safe environment. You also have a responsibility to ensure that your actions do not pose a risk to anyone else. I have mentioned a few scenarios above in relation to first aid and reporting accidents and the importance of making sure, as far as is possible, that an accident will not happen again.

There is a difference between a hazard and a risk. A hazard is something that can cause injury or ill health. The risk is the level of injury which results.

You can control a hazard by:

> Removing it altogether.
> Reduce the risk (e.g. put something in a safer place).
> Protect from the risk (e.g. guards on machines or warning signs and barriers).

Sometimes you can put things right yourself. For instance, you can pick up that plastic wrapping and put in the bin. You can make sure that when you put your bag down you tidy away the straps. Rucksacks and laptop/messenger bags pose a huge risk of slips, trips, and falls, which are the main causes of accidents and time off work.

Keep your own workstation or work area clean and tidy. Don't leave tools or sharp object hiding under other things. Someone can come along and injure their hand if they go to pick up something and catch themselves on the sharp object underneath.

Make sure that you clean your equipment after use so that it works properly. Make sure that you turn off electrical equipment when you have finished with it e.g. a drill or saw. I have seen some nasty accidents in young apprentices who have been careless and ended up with a nasty cut across the palm of their hand.

Make sure that you close drawers after use and not leave them open for someone to trip over.

Your employer will carry out the main risk assessment but here is a brief explanation of what it entails.

A **hazard** is anything that can cause harm. In addition to the above, it could be a chemical substance, something electrical, equipment like ladders etc.

The **risk** is how great the chance that someone will be harmed is. What would be the severity of the injury?

Your **employer** has a responsibility to ensure that the working environment is as safe as possible. You as an **employee** have a responsibility to comply with all instructions and safe practices and not do anything, which could endanger yourself or others.

If you see something that could harm others—do something about it. Do not leave it to someone else. The next time someone slips, trips or falls, it could be fatal!

Task:

Take a look around your **work area** or **office** and complete the checklist where it applies to your own work situation. You might be surprised at the results. Then complete the checklists.

- ➢ Is the screen on the computer adjusted to the right angle? Y/N
- ➢ Does the sunlight or electric light cause a glare making it hard to see? Y/N
- ➢ Can you tilt the keyboard? Y/N
- ➢ Is your chair comfortable? Y/N
- ➢ Is it the right height? Y/N
- ➢ Does it support your back? Y/N

- Do you sit in it properly or are you perched on the edge? Y/N
- Can you adjust it? Y/N
- Have you? Y/N
- Is there enough space to push it back without obstructing a walkway? Y/N
- Is your workstation/desk the right height? Y/N
- Are the edges smooth or are their sharp edges and corners that need fixing? Y/N
- Is it the right size? Do you have enough room for everything without clutter? Y/N
- Is it in the way of other people wanting to get past? Y/N
- Is all your equipment stored safely e.g. scissors, knives, staplers? Y/N
- Are all your papers organised safely and neatly? Y/N
- Is the telephone easily reached, or is it on a shelf, which is difficult to reach? Y/N
- Are shelves secured? Y/N
- Are they stacked too high causing a hazard and risk of things falling off onto someone's head or damaging the contents? Y/N
- Are they the right height? Y/N
- Do the filing cabinets cause an obstruction? Y/N
- Are they clear on top or have storage boxes and other items been put up there 'out of the way'? Y/N
- Do the drawers open easily? Y/N
- How many drawers can be open at once? Should only be one.

- ➢ Are wires and leads on electrical equipment frayed or trailing? Y/N
- ➢ Are there too many plugs in the socket? Y/N
- ➢ Is the lighting of a sufficient level or do you struggle to see? Y/N
- ➢ Do any of the light bulbs need changing? Y/N
- ➢ Do you have a heater? Y/N
- ➢ Does it work? Y/N
- ➢ Does it give out enough heat? Y/N
- ➢ Are there adjustable controls? Y/N

Can you add anything else to the list?

Now take a look at some other hazards and risks which you might find on the premises. Add anything not listed.

Electricity and electrical appliances	
Y/N	Exposed wires in flexes or frayed coverings
Y/N	Broken or blackened sockets
Y/N	Defective plugs
Y/N	Exposed wires in flexes or frayed coverings
Y/N	Unreported, un-repaired equipment
Fires and flammable substances	
Y/N	Fire exit doors locked or blocked
Y/N	Fire exit doors wedged open
Y/N	Waste bins used as ash trays
Y/N	Overloaded sockets
Y/N	Papers piled near electrical equipment or sockets
Y/N	Poor ventilation
Y/N	Furniture too near fires

Halls /staircases/landings

Y/N	Clutter on stairs
Y/N	Boxes or other obstructions in corridors
Y/N	Worn or frayed carpets
Y/N	Poor lighting in dark conditions
Y/N	Wet or slippery floor surfaces
Y/N	Furniture placed in walkways

Chemicals or toxic substances

Y/N	Using toxic substances in poorly ventilated rooms
Y/N	Inadequate steps ladders for reaching high shelves
Y/N	Uneven flooring
Y/N	Wet or slippery floors i.e. in the toilets
Y/N	Broken furniture

Other Hazards

Y/N	Accidents with incorrectly stored pieces of equipment, i.e. staplers, scissors, knives
Y/N	Boxes and packets haphazardly stacked
Y/N	
Y/N	

Anything not listed

Y/N	
Y/N	
Y/N	
Y/N	
Y/N	

(Source CE1/97)

An excellent website to browse around in general is http://www.worksmart.org.uk/rights/health_and_safety

Responsibilities for security in the workplace.

There is a vast difference in the size of organisations and types of businesses. All have their own security procedures.

Security in the workplace covers two important aspects.

1. Security of premises.

2. Security of information.

Security of premises.
These procedures may be as simple as who is given responsibility for locking up at night. On the other hand, there may be signing-in procedures or even showing your identity at the gate before you even get onto the car park or entrance.

Designated key holders normally hold keys. Often a key holder may have just the keys that relate to the job/position. In smaller premises, a key holder may hold all the keys. In a cash office, security is usually tight and often it takes two people to have access to certain areas such as the safe. It is important that keys are signed in and out and a register kept of who holds which keys.

Certain people will have access to the alarm codes. If at some point, in the case of holidays for instance, you are given temporary responsibility for setting the alarm and locking up, you must not divulge these codes to anyone at all, before, during, or after the period of responsibility. The same applies for permanent responsibility.

Whatever the procedures, it is important that you follow them. They are there for a reason; a breach of security can result in the loss of a lot of jobs if a competitor gets to know confidential company information, or there is a break-in with goods stolen.

Security of information.
No matter if you are in a workshop, factory, or office environment, there will be areas, and files, which are

restricted and marked 'confidential' or 'restricted'. You must respect these and abide by instructions.

If the wrong people have access to information, the results could be catastrophic, resulting in lost business.

When you started work, you were given the terms of your contract and these bind you. However, some things are so obvious they are not stated. Disclosing confidential information without authority could be a sackable offence or at least subject to sever disciplinary procedures. Information is often looked upon by the courts as property right and consent is needed for it to be disclosed.

So, no loose talk in the pub, club, gym, or anywhere else where you hang out, no matter how important it makes you feel to be able to share that information.

There are various types of documents such as letters, reports, e-mails, lists, newsletters, and spreadsheet and database printouts. With a newsletter or poster there would be a combination of graphics and text. Parts of a spreadsheet or database could be included in a report either in table form or with the use of a chart or graph. What may not appear to be of much importance to you may, in fact, be of great importance to someone else, especially a competitor.

Information therefore must be kept secure and not left lying around. Therefore, a health and safety discipline about keeping everything tidy also has implications for security. This applies to a job or project you may be working on and is tangible i.e. it can be seen. It also applies to computerised information which is often password protected. Do not under any circumstances share your password or let anyone see what you input into the computer.

Confidentiality.

Data Protection was covered in *Skills for Employability Part One: Pre-Employment*. A brief re-cap will not go amiss.

The Data Protection Act 1998 lays down the rules for dealing with personal and sensitive information—both paper and computerised. Individuals are allowed by law to find out what information is held about them by organisations that, by law, have to follow the eight principles of good information handling.

"The act contains eight 'Data Protection Principles'. These specify that personal data must be:

Processed fairly and lawfully.

Obtained for specified and lawful purposes.

Adequate, relevant and not excessive.

Accurate and up to date.

Not kept any longer than necessary.

Processed in accordance with the 'data subject's' (the individual's) rights.

Securely kept.

Not transferred to any other country without adequate protection in situ."

(Source: http://dataprotectionact.org/1.html 07.03.2012)

The 'Data Controller' in an organisation is responsible for making sure that the organisation complies with the act.

How does this affect me as an employee?

The bottom line for you as an employee is that you have to make sure that you keep information, paper-based or computerised, safe and secure and not give out personal or sensitive information to anyone who does not have the authority to have it. Just because someone asks for information, does not mean they are entitled to have it.

The easy solution is to ask someone in authority if you are not sure.

The computer screen should not be in a position where anyone passing, and who should not have access to the information, can see the information on the screen. This includes visitors. Privacy screens are available.

One word of caution. Having jumped through all the hoops of searching for a job, sending your CV, going for interview etc you will be excited at having landed a job. It is tempting to chat away to friends in the pub or club or wherever it is that you socialise.

*Remember! **Loose** talk = **Lose** business!*

You never know who is listening or what the person you are talking to— even a friend—will do with the information, so one good rule of thumb is quite simple. Do not talk in detail about what you do or what your organisation does. Organisations keep information about employees and customers. The Data Protection Act 1998 protects individuals by regulating what types of information can be held by another. There is another set of regulations, which apply to confidentiality. The Privacy and Electronic Communications (EC Directive) Regulations 2003 were amended in 2011 in relation to the use of 'cookies' for storing information on websites and mobile devices. These regulations work with the Data Protection Act 1998. The Information Commissioner is responsible for enforcing the act. Go to the Information Commissioner's Office website: http://www.ico.gov.uk/ for more information.

Much of this should be covered at your induction but it is never too early to be aware of your responsibilities as an employee.'

(Skills for Employability Part One: Pre-Employment. Marsh. 2012 P108)

Task ✏️

What kinds of information would be confidential?

1.

2.

3.

Copyright.

'It is easy to search for images on the Internet and download them to your computer. But, beware! Before you use them, check that the pictures are not copyrighted.

You must have the owner's permission to use copyrighted work. If you look at the front of this book, there is a statement about the author's copyright. Copyright [written, theatrical, music or artistic work] lasts for the life of the creator plus seventy years from the end of the year of the author's death. After this, the work comes into what is known as 'the public domain'.

The UK and many other countries have signed up to the Berne Convention—the Universal Copyright Convention—which came into force in 1952 and amended in 1971. This means that these countries do not have to sign up for copyright protection as it is automatic.

"The law of copyright and its related rights in the UK can be found in the copyright sections of the Copyright Designs and Patents Act 1988 (as amended)."

More information at: http://www.ipo.gov.uk/types/copy/c-about.htm'

(Skills for Employability Part One: Pre-Employment. Marsh. 2012 P109)

Equal Opportunities

You should be made aware of your organisation's Equal Opportunities Policy.

This is a very involved subject but without getting political under the Equality Act 2010, it means that we are all equal and should not be treated any different because of sex, race, religion, or personal beliefs. In other words, 'it bans unfair treatment'.

Therefore, 'The Equality Act 2010 makes it unlawful for a company to discriminate against anyone on the grounds of race, sex, pregnancy and maternity, marriage or civil partnership status, gender reassignment, disability, religion or belief, age or sexual orientation'.

Other acts, which relate to this, are:

> ➤ The Sex Discrimination Act 1975 [SDA] (amended 1980), which makes it unlawful to discriminate on grounds of sex or marital status in recruitment, promotion, and training.

> ➤ The Race Relations Act 1976 [RRA] (amended 1994), which makes it unlawful to discriminate on grounds of race, colour, nationality or ethnic or national origin. This Act covers recruitment, promotion, and training.

> ➤ The Equal Pay Act 1970 (amended 1983) came into force in 1975. Designed to eliminate discrimination in pay between men and women. The 1983 amendments included work of equal value.

> ➤ The Disability Discrimination Act 1995 [DDA] (amended 2004). This contained employment sections that came into effect in 1996. Under the act, an employer has a duty to make 'reasonable adjustments' to premises and/or working practices, which will allow a disabled person to be employed. Disabilities could include physical and sensory

disabilities, learning difficulties, mental health problems. In addition, progressive conditions such as Multiple Sclerosis and Aids are included.

> The Human Rights Act 1998, which became law in 2000. They relate to the basic rights and freedoms to which everyone is entitled. Check out more on the web. http://www.equalityhumanrights.com/human-rights/

The definitions of the above acts are wide. This chapter is meant only to give an idea [to you the reader] of what could affect you in the workplace.

Codes of Practice.

Q. What is a code of practice?

This is quite a difficult term to explain. You may have seen one on some literature from your bank or one of the utilities such as your electricity or gas provider.

Put simply, it is a guide of what should be followed; a guide with which everyone in the organisation should comply.

A code of practice is a framework for minimum standards and good practice set by an organisation, an industry, or professional body. Individuals and companies will follow this code of practice (the way in which they will work) and usually provide their customers with a copy. Employees are therefore provided with a set of standards and procedures to which they must work in order to maintain quality standards. They often outline what action the organisation will take if there is a complaint.

The code of practice, which isn't law, may be in the Quality Manual or you may need to speak to your manager.

Ethical standards.

Q. What do we mean by the term 'ethical'?

This is another difficult term to explain. I looked it up on the web where there are some very detailed explanations. I also looked it up in my Collins dictionary, which explained:

'Ethical: relating to morals, moral principles, and rules of conduct. Some explanations from the web are 'theory or system of moral values; the rules or standards governing the conduct of a person or the members of a profession; a social, religious, or civil code of behaviour considered correct, especially that of a particular group, profession, or individual.' http://www.thefreedictionary.com/ethics

In other words, ethical is about doing the right thing, being fair and honest. It is possible to act within the law and still be unethical. It is about thinking about who is affected by your actions and decisions. One example I came across related to staff being paid low wages and the employers keeping tips from customers in order to boost profits. http://www.bbc.co.uk/schools/gcsebitesize/business/enviro nment/acompetitivemarketrev1.shtml

Personal Integrity.

Q. What do we mean by 'integrity'?

Again, we turn to the dictionary, which tells us that it is an *'adherence to moral and ethical principles; soundness of moral character; honesty'.* Most of us are honest and use integrity in our decisions. However, this is open to risk, especially if you are tempted to 'go with the flow'. In short, you need to be able to stand up for what you believe in and what is right even if you are the odd one out and going against the tide.

Compliance.

Compliance in the context of the workplace means that everyone has to comply or adhere to the laws, regulations, policies, and procedures, which apply to your organisation.

The consequences of not doing so can be great and result in large fines or even prison. Your employer therefore must keep up to speed with laws, regulations, and statutory responsibilities, which affect the organisation and make sure that employees are aware of these. Everyone must comply with the law. Ignorance is no defence.

As I said earlier:

➢ Employees have rights and responsibilities.

But remember!
➢ Employers also have rights and responsibilities.

I have included a lot of web addresses in this chapter.

There are many good websites with more information, e.g., http://www.cepr.org/aboutcepr/policies.htm. Also, look at the section on useful links at the end of this book. Use them for reference and once you have read through the chapter, go back and explore further.

This chapter has been quite a lot to swallow. You might find it best to go back over it again. You do not need to know the legislation in-depth but you do need to be very aware of your responsibilities, especially in relation to health, safety, and security.

Re-cap.

In this chapter, you have learned about:

> ➢ Employment Rights and Responsibilities (ERR). That is *your* employment rights and *your* responsibilities for health, safety, and security in the workplace.

> ➢ Contracts of Employment.

> ➢ We also covered your *employer's* rights and responsibilities in these areas.

> ➢ The section on equal opportunities led into other areas of legislation, which are relevant to equal opportunities.

> ➢ Codes of Practice, ethical standards and personal integrity.

This knowledge will be invaluable to you when you move into employment. If you are due to attend for an interview, don't forget to emphasise that you have learned about these essential topics.

Check your knowledge.

Put the answer below without looking back on the chapter.

1. List three principles of the Data Protection Act 1998.

>

>

>

2. Why is it important not to discuss your job in detail or the work of your organisation?

3. Security of information is important. List three different ways in which information appears.

>

>

>

What is the consequence of loose talk in the pub or club etc.?

Now you can go back at check your knowledge.

Signposting to QCF.

Relationship of this chapter to the knowledge and understanding of other qualifications.

SSA 14.1 Foundations for Learning and Life.

14.2 Preparation for Work.

City & Guilds Awards and Certificates in Employability and Personal Development 7546.

> Effective skills, qualities, and attitudes for learning and work.

> Rights and responsibilities in the workplace.

> Introduction to health and safety awareness in the workplace.

> Health and safety in a practical environment.

> Individual rights and responsibilities.

> Health, safety, and security in the workplace.

> Valuing equality and diversity.

OCR Personal Life Skills.

> Forming personal relationships and understanding diversity.

> Understanding personal relationships and respecting diversity.

OCR Employability Skills.

> Learning about workplace values and practices.

Functional Skills English.

> Reading.

Essential Skills Wales Communication.

> Reading.

Chapter Two. Managing Your Money

You have landed a job. You work hard for the first week or month. You get your first pay packet. Wow! You feel rich. But hold on—there isn't as much going into the bank as you thought there would be.

In this chapter, we will look at the bottom line so to speak of a pay slip. We will look at ways of budgeting sensibly so that you are not running out of funds before your next payday or getting into debt.

Pay Slips.

- ➢ Income Tax.
- ➢ National Insurance (NI).
- ➢ Deductions.

You may be paid weekly or monthly so we will look at both and what information appears on your pay slip.

The tax year runs from April 6th one year to April 5th the next. Each organisation has its own format for the layout of a wage slip but in general, it should include the following:

- ➢ Wages/salary to date in this tax year.
- ➢ Wages/salary this week/month (Gross = before any deductions).
- ➢ Income Tax deductions.
- ➢ National Insurance deductions.
- ➢ Amount paid (nett = after deductions).

Deductions.

<u>Income Tax.</u>

Income Tax is due on the amount of pay left, after certain allowances have been taken off. The most common allowance is the Personal Allowance.

The Income Tax office, works out a Tax Code based on your allowances. These fit in with the Income Tax tables that your wages department will use.

For the tax year 2012-2013, the Personal Allowance is £8105. This means that you can earn £8105 in the tax year without paying income tax. To make this easier to manage I have put this into weeks. So £8105 divided by 52 (weeks) equals £155.87 per week. If you earn less than this, you should not have income tax deducted.

Your employer has special Income Tax tables to make sure that you pay the right amount. If you are paid monthly then the weeks in that month will be added together and the tax tables will tell your employer how much tax you should have paid up to the date you are paid, based on your earnings to that date. So for example, if you are paid monthly, you can earn £675.42 per month before paying any tax. (£8105 divided by 12).

As I have just said, these allowances versus the amount of tax due, add up each week/month. Therefore, if you have time off work for which you are *not* paid, this will show up and you will only pay tax on what is due that week/month based on what you earned.

This is important. You *must* check your pay slip. Mistakes do happen and it is your responsibility and yours alone to make sure that you are paying the right amount. Ignorance is no defence.

We will now look at Income Tax rates. The figures overleaf are for illustration only. I have taken the information on these tax rates and allowances from the website http://www.hmrc.gov.uk/rates/it.htm (HMRC means Her Majesty's Revenue and Customs.)

There are different rates depending on your income. In 2012-2013 on gross earning (before any deductions) of up to £34370 you will pay tax at a Basic rate of 20%.

Fig.1

	Weekly	Monthly(x4.33)	Annual(x52)
Gross	265.00	1148.33	13780.00
Less Allowance	-155.87	-675.40	-8105.00
Tax due on	109.13	472.93	5675.00
Tax @ 20%	**£21.83**	**£94.59**	**£1135.00**

The figure in **bold will** be deducted.

The figures are not exact—if you are checking— as they allow for rounding up or down when working to two decimal points.

Don't forget that one month is four weeks plus a few days. Every three months there is what we call a five-week month. It is important to allow for this in your calculations. If you divide a monthly salary by four weeks, you will have no money in the fifth week of a five-week month! On the other hand—if you are paid weekly and you could be a little in pocket on that fifth week as everything is taken care of over four weeks.

Depending on your circumstances, there are also some allowances on top of the one quoted which could bring down your tax bill.

National Insurance.

Everyone of school-leaving age is given a National Insurance number. This in effect identifies who you are and is unique to you. The number is made up of two letters followed by six numbers followed by one letter. e.g. XX 12 34 56 Y. It never changes. It is your own personal number and you must not give it out carelessly or put it on a CV for example. There are however, some people to whom you must give your number. These include your employer, HM Revenue and Customs, Department of Work and Pensions, your local council if you are claiming Housing Benefit, your bank if you open an Individual Savings Account (ISA).

'You pay National Insurance contributions if you are an employee or self-employed and you are aged 16 or over, as long as your earnings are over a certain level.'

www.hmrc.gov.uk/ni/intro/basics.htm#4 sourced 23.05.2012

There are different rates of contribution depending on whether you are employed or self-employed. We are looking at you as an employee and a simple example. They can be quite complicated but I will just give the bare bones here, as up-to-date information is readily available on the HMRC website above.

The amount you pay is calculated on your gross wage/salary i.e. before any income tax is taken out. There is a figure below which you do not pay, but are given a credit for pension purposes. There is also an upper earnings limit, over which you pay a reduced rate.

'If you are employed you pay Class 1 National Insurance contributions. The rates for 2012-2013 at the time of writing are:

1. if you earn more than £146 per week and up to £817 a week, you pay 12 percent (%) of the amount you earn between £146 and £817.

2. if you earn more than £817 per week, you also pay 2 per cent (%) of all your earnings over £817.

You pay a lower rate if you're a member of your employer's contracted-out pension scheme.

Your contributions are deducted from your wages by your employer.' www.hmrc.gov.uk/ni/intro/basics.htm#4 sourced 23.05.2012

We will now show this as an example of what you might have deducted from your wages.

Fig 2.

	Weekly	Monthly(x4.33)	Annual(x52)
Gross	265.00	1148.33	13780.00
Less N.I.Allowance	-146.00	-632.67	-7592.00
NI contribution due on	119.00	515.66	6188.00
@ 12%	**£14.28**	**£61.94**	**£742.56**

A Pay Slip Example.

Now to go back to pay slips. Below is a simplified version of what it could look like.

Fig 3.

Week ending 13/04/2012	Week No 2 (The second week in the tax year)	NI Number XX 12 34 56 Y
Pay to date		**Pay this week**
£530.00		£265.00
Tax to date	Tax (Fig 1)	*-£ 21.83*
43.66	Gross less I. Tax =	£243.17
NI to date	NI (Fig 2)	*- 14.28*
28.56	Gross less NI	£228.89
	Other deductions	Nil
	Nett pay	**£228.89**

In the next example (**Fig 4.**), we are looking at a monthly pay slip so the tax calculation period will be different.

Month ending 30/04/2012	Period 1 or April (The first month in the tax year)	NI Number XX 12 34 56 Y
Pay to date		**Pay this month**
£1148.33 *(1st month of tax year)*		£1148.33
Tax to date	Tax (Fig 1)	*-£ 94.59*
94.59	Gross less I.Tax =	£1053.74
NI to date	NI (Fig 2)	*- 61.94*
61.94	Gross less NI	£991.80
	Other deductions	Nil
	Nett pay	**£991.80**

For illustration only.

All payslips are different. If you are not clear, do not quite understand all the figures or think that there has been a mistake, ask your wages department to clarify. **Not** your manager or supervisor or worse—a colleague. Your wages and your pay slip are your personal business and confidential. In any case, it could cause a problem if the person you are asking advice from finds out that you are being paid more than they are!

If you think you have not been paid overtime or the right hours etc, then you could perhaps speak to your supervisor/manager who will check the time sheets. It may however, be company procedure to check with the wages department.

Budgets.

You have just seen from the examples above, that what looked like a comfortable wage has been whittled down due to deductions.

Some of the topics following may seem obvious to you or you may be doing something similar already. If so—good. You are managing your money. However, if you have recently moved from home where everything was done for you and have moved into your own flat or house, it will come as a shock when bills roll in and you hadn't realised how much it actually costs to live, even simply.

When you are working out your weekly/monthly outgoings, it is common to look at the obvious ones like rent, mortgage, gas, electric, council tax etc. and spend the rest on food and entertainment. After all, after a hard week in work you want to relax and chill out.

But what about all the other bills that sneak up on you? For instance water rates, house insurance, vehicle tax and insurance, an allowance for vehicle repairs & maintenance, telephone, mobile phone, newspapers/magazines. Some are weekly expenses, some are monthly expenses, some are annual expenses. Annual expenses can be a big problem if you don't budget properly.

Before we go further, I would like to explain that I am speaking from experience. As a newly married couple, we did a mental approximate calculation of expenses. Then one day the electricity bill arrived! There was a quick scrabble around for every halfpenny, penny, and any other coin we could find! From then on, we kept a very, very detailed budget and over the years, it has worked. When there has not been a lot left for treats, at least we knew that we could pay the bills, be fed and be warm—the absolute essentials.

May I share with you an example of what I did? From experience, I found it best to turn all the weekly and monthly expenses into an annual figure and then work out how much, realistically, we needed to survive and not get into debt. Either how much a week we needed (weekly wage) or how much a month (monthly wage as times changed).

Another piece of advice: if you are paid a basic plus regular overtime, work on the basic and regard overtime as extra to meet other things that pop up. Overtime has a habit of disappearing if business falls off.

Task .✐

On the worksheet on the next page, write down all of the regular expenses you can think of.

If you can think of anything else, add it in. I have given you some blank rows.

Expense	Weekly/monthly /annual	Annual figure
Rent	weekly x 52 =	£
Gas	monthly x12 =	£
Electricity	monthly x12 =	£
Vehicle Tax	Annual =	£
Vehicle Insurance	Annual =	£
Vehicle repairs	Annual =	£
Telephone	monthly x12 =	£
Mobile	monthly x12 =	£
Holidays (keep in bank acc.)	weekly x 52	£
Food/ toiletries	weekly x 52	£
Newspaper/Mags.	weekly x 52	£
House Insurance	Annual	£
Spending Money	weekly x 52	£
Fares to work	weekly x 52	£
TV Licence		£
Total		**£**

Next, add up all the annual expenses.

These are your annual outgoings. Most bills are paid by direct debit now, on a monthly basis from your bank account.

If you are paid weekly, divide the total by 52.

If you are paid monthly, divide the total by 12.

Because you are working an annual figure, this is how much you need to keep at one side before working out if you can afford any extras. There should be enough building up to pay the bills.

If you are paid in cash, only keep what you need each week for paying things in cash and put the rest in the bank. If you are paid into the bank, then only draw out what you need for cash payments such as food/toiletries, spending money, magazines/papers etc.

Tip.
It used to be that all wages were paid in cash and at home you would see different tins in the drawer or on the mantelpiece for the rent man, milkman etc. With a virtually cashless society, this has all but disappeared. However, this does not stop you having 'virtual compartments' in your cash book. For instance, if you allow £10 per week for car repairs, keep a little column in your cashbook to keep track of this when money is spent on repairs/tyres etc., as these are not regular expenses.

Do not make the mistake of thinking that your bank balance is looking healthy and you can blow it all on a night out.

What will happen if you do this and you have forgotten that your house insurance renewal is due, (annual payment)?

Panic Stations! That is what will happen!

If you have spare money each week/month over and above your regular expenses, keep a record of what you are spending out of it. Another 'virtual box'!

Credit Cards and Bank Cards.

A bank card (or debit card) allows you to draw cash out from your bank account or pay for goods and services at the point of sale—as long as there is money in your account. It is easy to get carried away! All transactions will show up on your bank account statement at the end of the month. It is important to check all the credits and debits to make sure that there are no mistakes or that you have forgotten to allow for something.

In the last chapter, we talked at length about security of information and confidentiality. There is another aspect to confidentiality for which you alone are responsible. Below are a few simple steps to prevent you becoming the victim of fraud or identity theft.

Some security essentials with the use of cards.

Personal Identification Numbers (PIN).
When you are issued with a credit card or bank card, you are issued with a Personal Identification Number, or PIN, which enables you to draw money from a cash machine or buy goods. You may change this to a number of your choice but—and I can't emphasise this enough—keep it safe and do not disclose it to anyone.

Passwords.
Your bank will also send a password with your debit card. This is for use on the Internet. Internet banking is a good way to keep track of your transactions to make sure that everything that should go in and out has done so. Again, keep this password safe. Change it to one of your choosing if you like. Instructions from banks are "never to write them down". Personally, this is hard considering how many different passwords you need for various websites. However, if you use something unique to you, you should have no trouble remembering it. Try not to use your phone number or date of birth, as they are obvious and easy to work out if your card is stolen or misused.

Checking statements.
Keep all your receipts at least until your statement comes through. Check it thoroughly and report any discrepancies. Only then should you consider destroying your receipts. If you do, use a shredder. Of course some obvious ones, like those for larger purchases, should be kept.

Disposing of receipts and old statements.
How long you keep receipts and statements is up to you. However, it is best to use a shredder. This will avoid your personal details being found on a rubbish tip!

Internet banking (or online banking.
This is a popular method of banking. Transactions are much simpler. However, it is useful and I would say, important, that you keep some sort of manual or computerised record of your spending. I once had a computer which came with software for a money management programme. It was super duper and tied up with my bank statement. However, I abandoned it when the computer crashed and all the information was lost. It was actually time-consuming and I set up a spreadsheet to do the same job. Again, this was time-consuming, but in the interest of domestic harmony, I find a spreadsheet is invaluable for the budget with a manual record being sufficient for the day-to-day over budget transactions. In this way, I can check quickly if something has gone through or not.

Security in online banking.
- Do not add the website of your bank as a favourite or bookmark in your browser.
- Always type in the full address of your bank.
- Never respond to e-mails asking you to enter your online banking details or confirm your account details. Banks have strict security procedures for contacting customers in the case of account problems.
- Keep your log on details safe.

Card storage.
Be careful where you store your cards. Do not have your purse or wallet on view or in the back pocket of your jeans where someone could just pull it out. Do not leave your purse of wallet lying around. In work, if you have a locker make sure that you use it.

Credit Cards.

Again, credit cards allow you to pay for goods or services. Sometimes there is a transaction charge; made by the seller, to cover what they say *they* are charged by their bank.

When the credit card statement comes in, check it against all the receipts, which of course, you have saved. Haven't you? The statement will have a date by which at least a minimum payment must be made to the credit card company. If you are budgeting correctly and have kept a record of what you have spent (over and above your regular outgoings), you should be able to pay the bill off in full.

Make sure that you allow enough time for the money to go from your account to the credit card company's account. Four working days is actually six if there is a weekend in the middle. If you pay in full, there is no interest payable. If you make a mistake and pay even a few pence short, you will be charged interest on the whole balance due. That would be quite a shock. You can pay in monthly instalments but this is very costly as the interest rate is usually quite high.

Be careful with your card. If you can't be careful, ask yourself if you could do without it if it is lost. Could you afford to pay for any bills that someone who uses it without your permission, could run up?

Store Cards.

These are called charge cards because you have an account, which is charged to the store—not your bank account or credit card account. Again, the same care and disciplines, which I have talked about earlier, apply. If you do have a store card, make sure that you keep a record of the transactions. Because they are not on your credit card statement or your bank account, it is easy to forget about them.

Savings.

Try to save something each month. If you have set up a budget along the lines I have illustrated above or you have a system which suits you, you will probably find that you are able to save a small sum each week—even if only £10.00.

Open a savings account and either pay in each week/month or set up a standing order at the bank so that money is transferred automatically. It actually becomes a fixed outgoing, which you can forget about while the money just grows and grows.

There are many types of savings accounts but the most tax efficient is an Individual Savings Account or ISA. You can pay in (invest) up to a certain allowance each year. This is set by the government. Usually ISA's attract a reasonable rate of interest. There is no tax due on the interest earned, which is why they are called 'tax-efficient'. A search on the Internet will bring up a huge choice of current deals. Alternatively, you can speak to a Customer Advisor in your bank or building society.

Re-cap.

This chapter has again been quite in-depth and I hope that you have enjoyed it and found it useful.

> ➢ You have learned about what you should find on your pay slip and how to understand it. This included Income Tax and National Insurance deductions.

> ➢ You have learned some ideas and strategies for budgeting.

> ➢ You have learned about the different types of cards or 'plastic' as they are sometimes called. Also about keeping cards safe.

Check your knowledge.

Put the answer below without looking back on the chapter.

1. Why is it important to understand your pay slip?

2. Why is it important to understand your money?

3. What would happen if you did not allow for the extra week, which falls four times a year (three monthly)?

4. Why is saving money a good idea?

Now you can go back and check your knowledge.

Signposting to QCF.

Relationship of this chapter to the knowledge and understanding of other qualifications.

SSA 14.1 Foundations for Learning and Life.

14.2 Preparation for Work.

City & Guilds Awards and Certificates in Employability and Personal Development 7546

> ➢ Managing personal finance.

> ➢ Managing own money.

> ➢ Personal money management.

OCR Personal Life Skills.

> ➢ Identifying, understanding, making, and managing risk in personal decision-making.

OCR Employability Skills.

> ➢ Learning to be financially capable.

Functional Skills English.

> ➢ Reading.

Essential Skills Wales. Communication.

> ➢ Reading.

Chapter Three.
The Business Environment

What do we mean by the business environment? We are not looking at the environment as a whole but the workplace and normal day-to-day business.

You may not be working in an office, which is what many perceive as being the 'business environment'. You may be working in a factory or on the shop floor of a manufacturing works. All organisations have an office of some sort, as this is where all the 'other side' of your work takes place. It is where calls from customers come in, where your pay slips are made up, where orders are agreed and finalised. Therefore, every department is part of the business and everyone has to work as part of a team in that particular business environment.

In *Skills for Employability Part One: Pre-Employment*, we touched on working relationships. Just for a minute, we will re-cap on that as you may have forgotten it or perhaps did not read Part One.

Re-cap.

'You may say: "I know how to work with other people. I mean, we stand there and chat and take our time with jobs. We have a great laugh. Sometimes, I am a bit late but my pals cover for me until I sneak in."

Right? Wrong! Of course, it is important that you enjoy your work but there is more to it than that. Working effectively in the workplace, starts when your alarm bell goes off in the morning, or someone calls you that it is time to get up.

It is important that you work effectively with your colleagues and supervisors, otherwise orders would not be met. Customers would be lost and, in the end, your employer would not be able to pay your wages.

You would not have a job anymore. You must be able to show that you are a reliable employee. How do you do this?'

If you haven't already read *Skills for Employability Part One,* I would encourage you to do so. Otherwise, we will need to go over the whole chapter again and we really need to build on that.

In this chapter, you will learn about working effectively for business success, which includes:

- ➤ Attitude and behaviour
- ➤ Communication
- ➤ Feedback on performance.
- ➤ Personal development
- ➤ Grievance and Disciplinary Procedures.

Attitude and Behaviour.

We will now look at acceptable levels of attitude and behaviour. We looked briefly at this important topic in *Skills for Employability Part One: Pre-Employment.* We looked at being flexible in work; your behaviour; following codes of conduct; being professional; motivation and your approach and attitude.

'If you show a willingness to do whatever task you are given, ask for more work when you have done the tasks given, are friendly and helpful, then you will please your employer/supervisor and soon become a valuable member of the team. You may be given more responsible work to do, along with more pay. That means more goodies in life—nice clothes, holidays, better place to live etc. More importantly, you will have a feeling of achievement and self worth which can only be good for your confidence and self-esteem.

It is hard starting at the bottom or taking a job which you think is beneath you but we all had to start somewhere and sometimes— especially in the case of temporary jobs—it is a kind of long interview so that the firm can see if you fit in. So be positive and look to the future. Be a 'Winner' and look up to where you are going.'

(Skills for Employability Part One: Pre-Employment. Marsh 2012 P45.)

That sometimes means taking on duties on a temporary basis for which you may not have an adjustment in pay. Look on this as a new experience to add to your portfolio. You sometimes have to work at the level to which you want to be and prove yourself before you are given more responsibility on a permanent basis.

*'A **Winner** is responsible for more than his/her job.*

A Loser says "I only work here".'

(Extract-Release Your Potential: Making Sense of Personal and Professional Development. Marsh 2011 P.5)

Communication.

Communication is essential. Without it, none of us can function. That is why communication is part of Functional Skills—English,which is now embedded in all learning programmes in schools. (In Wales, this is called Essential Skills Wales—Communication.)

It is essential that you are aware of how important your part in communicating effectively in the workplace is, whether it is verbal or non-verbal communication. This may be by speaking to someone on the telephone, speaking to someone face-to-face, sending an e-mail or letter, or leaving a message on the telephone. If you are shy and nervous, you may mumble and rush things. The effect of this is that the message does not come across clearly.

There are some simple tips and tricks to increase your confidence:

> ➢ Be professional and put on your company hat so to speak. You are the face of the company—leave the shy, nervous you at the door.
> ➢ Gather all the information you need before you make a call or send a message.
> ➢ Have a notepad to hand and a pen or pencil so that you can make notes. Keeping the caller waiting while you go to look for a pen or

something to write on does not create a good image of either yourself or the organisation.

➤ Before you answer the telephone, take a deep breath and remain cool, calm, and collected. The three 'C's' we talked about in Part One.

If you do this, you will stay in control, come across as professional and you will feel more confident. With practice, this confidence will become second nature.

How you speak is important. The tone of your voice is important, as is the language you use. You must not be over familiar with people but this does not mean that you cannot be friendly. You will be a bit more formal with people you do not know but when you have spoken to a person, a few times you may find that you are adopting a more informal approach as you deal with them.

On the telephone, remain calm even if you are dealing with a hostile caller. You do not have to take abuse from anyone. If you find that this is happening and you can't calm them down, politely put the caller on hold and find your supervisor. Listen to the callers concerns and be positive. If you can't offer a solution, tell them that you will pass the problem on to your supervisor (or whichever department could deal with the problem), and be sure to take down their name and telephone number along with details of the problem.

When answering the telephone, your organisation may have a set spiel or phrase which you must use when you answer. A short, curt 'Hello' barked down the telephone does *not* go down well with anyone. Make sure that you know your organisation's telephone number!

Your frame of mind actually shows in the tone of your voice. If you are cheerful while you answer the telephone or write a letter/e-mail, then it will come through in the tone of the communication. Put a smile into your voice and it will come through in the communication.

Try saying the word **YES** in different ways.

Does it come across as a **YES** or as a **NO?**

Does it say?

In verbal communication, you need to consider:

> ➤ Are you speaking too softly? If the person at the other end has to ask you to repeat yourself, they will get fed-up and could put the phone down or ask to speak to someone else.

> ➤ Are you speaking too loudly? It can come across as aggressive.

> ➤ Are you gabbling? We have all made a telephone call and the receptionist rattles off the usual '*Good Morning. Ac....Com..Mell..speaking. How n I h..u?* Think about it. Your first impression is not a very good impression is it and you start on the wrong foot.

Speaking to quickly means that the person at the other end can't understand you and, again, has to ask you to repeat yourself. This is a cause of nervousness and losing confidence. If this does happen, apologise, take a deep breath to calm yourself and repeat yourself, but this time, pronounce each word more slowly and clearly so that the person at the other end can understand you and leaves with a good impression of both you and your organisation.

Your body language is important as well and is a form of non-verbal communication. When you are talking to someone, remember that their space is theirs. You might be very tactile and see nothing wrong in touching someone. This may be very offensive to the other person. By all means, shake their hands when saying good-bye. That is polite and professional and leaves a good impression.

When writing a letter or sending an e-mail or text, the tone of your voice and your attitude come through in what you write and the way in which you write it. Check it over and if possible, put it to one side and come back to it later—especially if you are angry at something.

Contributing to discussions.
A discussion in the workplace may be very informal such as when your boss stops you in the corridor or in the workshop and wants to discuss a procedure or the progress of a job.

On the other hand, it may be a more formal meeting where other people on the team/other departments are present as well.

Whatever the occasion it is important that you:

> ➢ Make relevant contributions. These may be short or more extended.

> ➢ Prepare for a more formal meeting/discussion so that you can make a relevant and worthwhile contribution.

➤ Make different types of contribution, e.g., you may have to make a more in-depth point about something that could affect your department or organisation. Or you may be simply agreeing who will be responsible for what.

➤ Present your points of view and information clearly in a way that is suitable to the situation. A more formal meeting requires that you be a little more formal whereas an informal meeting could be more relaxed. This does not mean however that you are not professional.

➤ Listen to others' points of view and consider them as having equal value to anything that you want to say. It is important then, that you prepare for a meeting/discussion if you know about it in advance and have your notes ready so that you can keep to the point.

If the discussion is an informal one, of the kind I mentioned earlier, this would probably be about the work you are carrying out or a project you are working on and you should have most of the information in your head or, at your fingertips as it were. You could always ask to be excused for a minute in order to collect a file on the subject. No one will mind this.

Whatever type of meeting/discussion, your contributions must be of the sort that can move the discussion forward, which they will if they are relevant and open up a new area.

Writing.
In *Skills for Employability Part One: Pre-Employment,* we dealt with quite a lot on communication and various types of written communication.

Short talks and presentations.
A presentation is where the verbal and non-verbal come together. By presentation, we really mean a formal presentation of some facts, which you have researched. This

will involve using some sort of visual aid such as a flip chart, a Power Point presentation through a video overhead projector (OHP) or any other method in the rapidly expanding range of digital aids.

A short talk can be formal or informal. It may be that you have to stand up in front of a group and talk about something for a few minutes. It could also be something as simple as explaining a process to your supervisor in an informal setting such as the office or the workshop.

In any case, it is essential that you follow the rules above about being clear and structured. You will need to have all your information to hand for reference but you should not read from your notes. That is simply reading—not giving a talk.

You will need to adapt the talk or presentation to suit the people attending and the setting. I am a member of a number of networking groups and on occasion have been asked to speak. This could be a two to three minute slot or a more lengthy ten minutes.

Preparation is the key as it is important that you get the message across clearly and without waffle. I am not going to go into this here, as it will deviate from the topic of the chapter.

Barriers to communication.
The main barrier to communication is you. Your behaviour and how you act.

Do you have a prejudice about someone? We are all equal but not all the same. It is our differences that make up the richness of our country. Any prejudices you may have will most surely come across in the tone you use—whether it is written (non-verbal) communication or in speech (verbal communication).

Are you stressed? You know the scene, you have problems at home, you have a problem with a work colleague, and you are doing the work of two people. You are stressed! Take a few calming breaths and leave your problems at one side while you concentrate confidently on the 'communication' task. Otherwise, this stress comes through in a negative way.

Your contribution will be effective and help to maintain a happy and productive working relationship, which in turn will add to your confidence.

Points to remember.
Some things to remember in communication are the KISS and ABC methods:

Keep it short and simple

It

Short &

Simple

and

Accurate

Brief and

Concise

Also, think about the six questions that you must ask yourself.

WHO are you talking to?

WHAT information is relevant?

WHY are you communicating?

WHERE will you send the information?

WHEN will you send it? Now or can it go later?

HOW will you communicate? Telephone? Letter? e-mail? Discussion? Face-to-face?

Be clear and sensible with enough detail while remembering the **KISS** principle.

Speak properly. The level of formality/informality depends on the situation but at all times remain professional.

By all mean use the computer spell-checker but do not rely on this. Using a dictionary is a basic skill, which you need in order to function. The computer may well say a word is spelt correctly but it may be the wrong word. A dictionary gives the meaning so that you can be accurate in the words you choose. (You do know your ABC don't you?) I am not being insulting here but speaking from experience in working with adult learners who never actually mastered the alphabet! I cannot emphasise this too much. If the letter is very important, you may have to run it past your supervisor or manager. Before you do this—use a dictionary. Even the smallest workshop has a corner designated for office work. Make sure that a dictionary is an essential tool in the desk drawer. Not all offices are slick, smart ones. In retail in particular, space is dead money as space is for stock, which can make money.

Check point!
What is verbal communication?

Give two types of non-verbal communication.

Why is it important that you speak clearly on the telephone?

Why is it important to check your spelling?

Why is it important to check that you have used the correct word?

Feedback on performance.

Generally, we have an idea of what we want out of life. Some of us are more focused than others. While some people are happy to take life at a slower pace, some of us want to forge ahead and reach for the stars. As I said earlier, we are all equal but are not all the same. This is true of how we grow and develop.

In the workplace, you may be fortunate to be in an organisation that has planned learning and development opportunities for their employees built into their business plan. However many do not. What you will most certainly find is that you will be told if you have made a mistake.

On the other hand, you may well find that you are not often told when you have done a good job. When you have worked hard and tried hard to do a good job or reach a deadline this is very demoralising. Remember that when you reach the lofty heights of being a boss!

Feedback comes in two ways:

> - Formal feedback
> - Informal feedback

Formal feedback.
Apart from having some feedback on your performance *if* you do something wrong, you may be lucky enough to work for an employer who holds an annual appraisal of your performance.

You will most likely want to move forwards in life so that you can achieve your goals and see your dreams come true. You will firstly need to have some idea of what you want to achieve and secondly be willing to improve your work, acquire more skills, and be given work that carries more responsibility. In this way, you will move upwards and onwards.

A formal feedback session can take many forms—depending on your organisation. The feedback however, should always follow a pattern of positive, negative, positive. We call this the 'sandwich effect'. If you are simply given negative feedback, you will become disheartened.

Whoever is giving you feedback should first tell you what you have done well before launching into the parts that need some improvement. This then should lead on to a more positive outcome by looking at areas where you can improve.

Informal feedback.

Your supervisor or even someone more senior may walk by.

'Thanks for that Joe, very useful information.' or 'We can always rely on you to finish the job on time', may be the comment.

It is nice that others often overhear this positive feedback. You have tried hard and now have a small glow of satisfaction. Your confidence increases and goes up another notch.

However, if the comments (feedback) are not positive, they really should be given in private. A normal reaction is for someone to say, 'Oh no! Not again!' and shake their head leaving you feeling pretty small. You hope that no one has overheard. Anything more should be done in private.

The importance of continuous development.

Unless you are very unusual (or have a very hectic social life!), after you have mastered a job for some time you start to become restless or bored if you have no new challenges or nothing else to attract your attention and interest. However, it can be quite one thing to know that you are restless and in need of a change and quite another to decide what to do about it.

The tendency, if you are not careful, is to either become stuck in a rut or to 'job hop' without first thinking through the implications. You could end up worse off than you are now!

A sensible process of continuous development means that you seriously consider the benefits and weaknesses of your current position and look at how you can improve yourself to take advantage of new opportunities, which will be to your benefit. These may mean staying with your current employer and devising a method of learning new skills to develop your potential or, if this is not possible, taking time to consider suitable alternatives.

Continuous development never stops. As you grow older and gain more skills and experience, your needs and wants will change again—and then again! You will continue to progress throughout your whole career.

Part of this process, however, is developing self-awareness and self-knowledge - and this can be a painful experience! In other words, you need to know what people think of your skills and abilities now and your strengths and weaknesses. But beware, it is marvelous when people praise and flatter; it is a different thing entirely when someone tells you that improvement is necessary.

Dealing with feedback.

So then what are the skills required to give feedback? How do you deal with unwelcome comments about your work? Of course, much of the way in which you receive feedback and comments on your work depends on the skills of the person actually giving the feedback.

It is easy to assume that your supervisor or manager actually knows how to do this in a sensitive and constructive way. Is this always the case though? Well, actually, unless that person has had training—in other words been given the tools— the answer could well be a resounding, 'No'.

If your supervisor or manager is new to his /her job, they may actually be a little nervous. However, some things to remember when you get into a position where you have people under you apply equally when you are receiving feedback on your performance.

- ➤ Feedback should be given in private.
- ➤ Feedback should follow 'sandwich' effect. That is positive, negative, positive. An example would be, 'I am pleased with your work to date; you have fitted well into the team. However, we have noticed that you are always a little late. This holds up the day's work as the team cannot start until everyone is there. You also spend too much time on your mobile phone. You may think that no one has noticed but it has been brought to my attention. Is there a problem at home that we can help with? (This may lead to a short discussion, which could be solved by some flexibility on both parts.) Well, as I said, your work in general is good but you do need to pull your weight a bit more. If there is some area where you need more training, we can provide that.'
- ➤ Feedback should be swift and to the point. No-one likes to be kept guessing.
- ➤ Feedback should not be personal but keep to the point. No nasty or hurtful remarks.
- ➤ Feedback should clear with examples of instances where you have gone wrong and how things are expected to be done.
- ➤ Feedback should actually be two-way with an opportunity to reply and explain fully.
- ➤ Feedback should end on a positive note with an agreement on how to deal with problems in the future, e.g., 'Don't moan and complain; come to me with your grievance before it festers and is blown out of proportion.'
- ➤ If the problem is a team issue, then the team as a whole should be given feedback without anyone being singled out.

Dealing with positive feedback.

If you are in the fortunate position to be praised at every turn, you may be tempted to brag about this in the staff room or canteen. Don't! The others will only think that you are a big-head with an outsize ego. It also is demoralising for others, which does not do much for a team spirit and will only make you unpopular. Some members of the team may be struggling and your bragging will only make them feel more useless than they may already be feeling, or really are. If someone asks you how thinks went. Just shrug and say that everything went fine. Don't let it go to your head as you may start to slack and fall down on the job.

We all have to learn and all can improve. Even though you may be doing well on current tasks, there will be a time when you have to learn a new skill and *you* may turn out to be the one struggling until you master it. Pride comes before a fall they say.

Dealing with negative feedback.

This is your first job or your first one for a long time and you are anxious to do well. Perhaps you have not picked up the skills as quickly as you might have done. In order to maintain quality—otherwise your organisation would lose its customers and ultimately have to cut jobs—you have to be told if something is not quite right, but do not focus solely on this, forgetting the positive things you have been told.

> ➢ It is nature to be self-defensive. Try asking for an example of what you have done wrong or how you could do thinks in the right way.
> ➢ Take the blame if the blame is yours. Don't pass the blame onto someone else. If you are being accused of something unfairly, discuss this and ask how you should have acted.
> ➢ If you really are in the wrong, accept it and, above all, learn from your mistake.

> If feelings are running high, it may be that a cooling-off period is needed. Ask if the interview can be held later. Perhaps it is just before your mealtime and you are in need of food and a break. After a break, or when you are not trying to meet a deadline would be better. Look at things from the other point of view.

> Some bosses rarely give praise. State your case clearly without getting upset or aggressive.

As I said earlier, your supervisor or boss may be new to his/her job and inexperienced in giving feedback. In which case, it is not easy for them either. However, if we only heard good things, none of us would improve or develop. This applies to organisations as much as individuals.

Constructive feedback.

A positive outcome of this session—whether formal or informal—may be that areas for improvement have been highlighted. This could apply to your work or to a learning programme you are undertaking as part of your skills training. Whatever feedback you are given, it must be constructive. If there is nothing to build on then it is a waste of time.

This means:

> You or the team should know as soon as possible how much progress you have made. This could be in quality standards, meeting targets, or customer satisfaction. This will motivate you.

> Identifying whether you are following the best way to achieve the task. If it is a learning programme, you will need to ask yourself if you are using the learning methods best for you.

> Identifying if the targets are SMART (specific, measurable, achievable, realistic, and time-constrained).

(Release Your Potential: Making Sense of Personal and Professional Development. Marsh 2012. P32.)

> Making sure that the work is not too hard or easy. If too hard, this may be a capability issue and more training needed or moving on to an easier task.

Personal development.

An organisation is only as good as its members. If an organisation is to grow and develop then its members must also grow and develop. In these times of fast-changing technology and business practices, no one can afford to stand still. I once wrote that 'standing still equates to going backwards'.

Therefore, not only for your organisation's business success but also for your own personal development, you have to be prepared to learn.

Task

Think back to a task or learning programme you have been given to do / or attend.

List two things you learned from this.

1.

2.

Can you think why this was?

Did you enjoy the activity? Y/N

Why was this?

Did you find this easy? Y/N

Why do you think this was?

For learning, either formal or informal, to take place there must be a change as a result of that learning.

What changes took place in you as a result of building on the feedback, which resulted in a learning process?

Whether your learning need was identified by you or your employer, you must be motivated by whatever activity or course you undertake. You have to feel committed inside to completing it. I know, if it is a 'must do' you will do it anyway but if you can enjoy it and feel that you are learning and progressing then you will stick at it and do better. Too often I have seen colleagues just skim the surface and not complete all the work they should and therefore not achieve and move further to being more effective and achieving their goals. Apart from anything else, it is a waste of time. Both yours and your employers.

So how do you identify what you need to learn in order to improve or progress?

There are six questions that you should ask yourself:

1. **WHO** will I learn with?
2. **WHY** do I need to learn?
3. **WHAT** will I learn?
4. **WHEN** will I learn?
5. **HOW** will I learn?
6. **WHERE** will I learn?

Task 🖉

Let's take question two. **WHY** do I need to learn?

Can you think of one or two reasons?

Put your answers below.

1)

2)

Motivation is related to a need. For learning to take place, you need to be motivated and there are various reasons for wanting to learn something, which will motivate you to completing the course.

- ➢ You might want to gain a qualification (specific knowledge).
- ➢ You might want to develop yourself and increase confidence.
- ➢ You might want to increase your job prospects.
- ➢ Learning could make you feel more independent. It could lead to a job, which will take you away from home and give you the confidence to do that.
- ➢ Learning can lead to a better job, better income, and better life.
- ➢ Quite simply a sense of achievement.

Now that you have identified and settled on what you need to learn to achieve your goals, either in your personal or work life, you have a few more things to think about.

Is there anything, which could affect your plans? For instance in question six you asked yourself, 'Where will I learn?' It is no use signing up for a course or class, which you can't get to in time because of distance, work schedule or transport problems.

You also need to think about your life and how you will manage your time. In *Release Your Potential: Making Sense of Personal and Professional Development,* there is an in-depth section on time management. So here, we will just break it down into three main areas.

Prescribed Time. e.g., go to work.

Maintenance Time. e.g., shopping, cooking, looking after yourself.

Discretionary Time. Time left over which you can plan how you want to spend it. Your study time will have to come out of this.

Planning your study time, both formal and informal, into your day is the only way. Learning doesn't just happen by itself. If you sign up to a fitness centre, you need to keep to the sessions. Otherwise, you will have wasted your hard-earned subscription money.

If your employer cannot offer in-house training for short courses, you will need to find out who offers the courses you want to do.

Further reading: *Release Your Potential: Making Sense of Personal and Professional Development.*

Disciplinary and Grievance Procedures.

You may make a mistake on a job or when dealing with someone. We all make mistakes but the important thing is that we learn from them. A mistake however, usually has to be investigated at some level.

An organisation will have procedures for dealing with things that go wrong. These are called Grievance and Disciplinary Procedures. If the situation warrants it or the mistake or problem is repeated you may be given a verbal warning which, if the problem persists (and it could be something like being late for work) then this will eventually lead to a written warning and then dismissal.

There is also another type of procedure, which can be used to sort out problems. These are called Capability Procedures. If for instance, you are asked to do something for which you have not been trained and are not competent to do, or have been trained but are making mistakes, it may be that you need further training. In other words, it could be a capability issue. You will need to make yourself familiar with these procedures. They should be part of your induction or you may be told where you can find the information. Some organisations have a Quality Manual with everything in it. It may be a hard copy in the staff room or office or it may be on the computer.

Most organisations have procedures for dealing with issues that go against policy and procedure. They will also have a procedure for dealing with what we call a grievance. It is important that you pay attention to these; they should be brought to your attention at your induction. Sometimes, if you are lucky, all the company documents will be held in a file called a Quality Manual, which should be available for all staff to read. Sometimes these policies and procedures are kept on the company internal website called an intranet.

In Chapter One, we covered in some detail Employment Rights and Responsibilities which included health and safety.

It is important to remember what you have learned and practice it as bad behaviour and carelessness can lead to accidents.

Personal behaviour.
Show a willingness to work, to work as part of a team, don't waste time, organise your tasks and help others where you can. Good personal behaviour, contributes to a good all round attitude and a good impression to others of your organisation. This can only be good for business success and, in the long run, yours.

Re-cap.

In this chapter, we have looked at:

> ➤ What you can expect to find in the business environment. This applies as much to a shop floor environment as it does to an office environment.

> ➤ Communication. Different types of communication such as verbal and non-verbal, and the importance of clear and accurate communication.

> ➤ Feedback, which included both informal and formal feedback and ways of giving and receiving feedback.

> ➤ Personal development as an outcome of feedback. If your organisation is to grow and develop, it must develop its range of tools. One of the most important tools, which it needs, is YOU. A workman is only as good as his tools and in the same way, an organisation is only as good as its personnel/workers. Teamwork is essential, as is a positive, can-do attitude.

Embrace any opportunities you have to access further learning and development.

Check Your Knowledge

Put the answer below without looking back on the chapter.

1. List three types of communication.

2. Name two barriers to communication

3. Why should employees and employers look to developing more skills?

4. Name three types of feedback.

Now you can go back and check your knowledge.

Signposting to QCF.

Relationship of this chapter to the knowledge and understanding of other qualifications.

SSA 14.1 Foundations for Learning and Life.

14.2 Preparation for Work.

City & Guilds Awards and Certificates in Employability and Personal Development 7546.

> Effective skills, qualities, and attitudes for learning and work.

> Supporting others.

> Contributing to a team.

> Developing own interpersonal skills.

> Developing personal confidence and self-awareness.

> Developing self for learning and work.

> Identity and cultural diversity

OCR Personal Life Skills.

> Forming relationships and understanding others.

OCR Employability Skills.

> Carrying out and learning from practical tasks set in a work context.

> Preparing for and learning from a work placement.

Functional Skills. English.

> Reading.

Essential Skills Wales. Communication.

Wider Key Skills Working with Others (Wales only).

Chapter Four. The Importance of Good Customer Service

In writing this chapter, I am aiming at a wide cross-section of employees, prospective or otherwise, so I will make the topics as general as I can.

You may think that customers *only* exist in a shop, or where someone has sold you something for which you may well have paid a lot of money.

Actually, you would be wrong. So, what is a customer?

What do we mean by Customer Service?

In this chapter, we will look at:

> The customer and customer service environment.
> Internal and external customers.
> Maintaining standards.
> How to deal with minor problems.

The customer and the customer service environment.

Organisations work hard to get customers. In fact, I would suggest that most organisations have customers in some shape or form. At the beginning of the chapter I asked, 'What is a customer?'

Task

What do you think? Put your thoughts below or use a notepad.

A customer is someone for whom you do something, e.g., carry out a task, sell something to, or provide a service. These are the backbone of the business and in turn, they expect and should receive good customer service. That is they expect an organisation to provide goods or services to meet their needs.

In order to keep their customers, organisations have to work even harder that they had to in getting them in the first place. After all, if you didn't receive the level of service, which you expect in your personal life, you would soon go elsewhere.

Our first thought in thinking of customers is, for instance, in a shop. However, organisations providing goods to another organisation have customers. That is the organisation, which is buying the goods or services provided by another.

If those goods or services, and this includes after-sales services, do not meet expectations, then they, the customer, will take their business elsewhere.

As you move into employment, you may find that you are in a car repair workshop. If this is part of a large organisation, there may be a dedicated service desk and you do not come into contact with the person on whose car you are working. On the other hand, you could be in a small garage where you deal with customers as and when they arrive to drop off their cars, pick them up, or come in to discuss a problem. In this scenario, you will have face-to-face contact with the customer.

In this scenario, you then become the face of the organisation as how you treat your customers is the only yardstick they have of how good the organisation is.

You may find that you are in an office where you do not actually see any of your customers. Contact may be limited and usually carried out by telephone.

In this scenario, again you are the face of the organisation, especially if you are the first person to whom the customer speaks.

You may however be working in, for instance, the fashion department of a large department store. Being new and possibly inexperienced, your job role does not actually mean that you are advising customers on outfits. Your main tasks are to move stock around and keep the rails tidy.

In this different scenario, you are actually, again, the face of the organisation; especially if a customer asks for help!

It is important at all times, that your personal presentation is spot on and that you greet your customers pleasantly and with a smile. It can be difficult, especially when your supervisor is on your back because the regional manager has telephoned to say he/she is on his/her way for an unplanned visit and the department has to look 105% spot on to organisation requirements. However, if the customer is not afforded 100% attention, not only could you lose that customer but all those who come into contact with him/her and get the tale of incompetence and uncaring attitude.

It would not be long before sales went down and you were out of a job!

Internal and external customers.

Your first perception is that only people from outside the organisation are customers. You would be wrong. We learned earlier that 'a customer is someone for whom you do something e.g., carry out a task, sell something to, provide a service for.'

Task

Think about your organisation, one you have worked in or the one you are moving in to. Your job role will involve carrying out certain tasks for either people within the organisation or people outside the organisation.

Think about the people for whom you are doing work.

1. Write down the task.

2. Write down the position of the person for whom you are doing the work.

3. Identify if they are internal or external customers.

I will give you an example.

Scenario: A colleague, in a lower position than myself, has asked for some help to complete a task. I work in the Cash Office but new stock came in later than expected and, for security reasons, it must be checked and put away before closing time.

1. The task is putting away stock. There is a deadline and must be completed.

2. The position of the customer (person asking for help) is Junior Sales Assistant.

3. Internal customer (inside the organisation but from another department).

Now you have a go. You can write below or use a notebook or sheet of paper.

Maintaining standards.

For an organisation to operate effectively, all parts must work together. Our external customers don't care *how* we keep the cogs in the wheel turning; they only care that when they need us, we provide an excellent customer service.

"Customer service is all about needs—on the one hand the needs of the customers and on the other, the needs of the organisation".

(How to Pass, page 62 in Certificate in Customer Service Level 2.Prescott/Shoemark. Yale College, 2005.)

To achieve customer satisfaction you need a mixture of knowledge and skills. In this chapter, we are not going to go too in-depth. If your job requires it, you will probably have some company specific customer service training. Here we are just looking to introduce you to what would be expected in any organisation when you join it.

It is important to the organisation and ultimately you for your future job prospects that you develop and maintain a good working relationship with your customers. This in turn develops the business as your customers come back time and again and, hopefully, recommend your organisation to others as being customer focussed and always being willing to go the extra mile in meeting the customer's needs.

We talked in Chapter One about codes of practice. Your organisation, especially if it is a large one, may well have written codes of practice. In other words, the standards which they expect to maintain. There will also be procedures for resolving complaints.

However, you may be working for a smaller organisation that does not have all this written down in a formal way. They will most probably however have some form of informal procedure to follow. The maxim is—if in doubt ask.

Task

Think back to an organisation you have worked in or have dealt with. This could be any organisation, even a college.

Q. What do you think are **their** perceptions of their customers? *Perhaps, you can tell this by the way in which you have been treated at some point.* Write your thoughts below.

Q. What are **your** perceptions of that organisation?

All organisations are fighting for a share of the business available.

In order for you to give the very best customer experience, you will need to know how far you can go in agreeing something to sort out a problem and when you have to have permission from someone. For example, if a customer is haggling for a large discount, you will probably have to get authority from the manager. Otherwise, you could be giving away all the profits with the result that there is no money to pay wages.

If, as we talked about earlier, you are the first person the customer talks to, you would be regarded as what we call 'front-line staff'. This could be a receptionist, sales staff, or someone in a call centre.

People in other departments who back up the work of the organisation are called support staff. This could be the service department of a car manufacturer, a service department who supplies parts or people in another department such as stock control or finance etc.

All these must work as a team as each gives an excellent customer service to the other so that the organisation at the top of the pile can function according to their quality standards.

Some of the skills needed are:

> Product knowledge.
> Communication skills—both verbal and written.
> How to address customers.
> Interpersonal skills. That is, how to interact with customers through body language, a pleasant manner, being friendly and supportive without being over-familiar.

Product knowledge.
A key to providing excellent customer service is to know your product. This can be as simple as knowing where to find products in a catalogue or on a computer. Eventually you will come to know these off by heart. Don't be negative and tell your customer that you can't find the information from the computer terminal where you are working. They don't want to know that. Be positive, apologise for keeping them waiting, and just say that you need to go to another screen or terminal. Go to one where you can or ask the customer to wait a moment while you find out the information from someone else who can access the system holding the information. In all cases, be positive and pleasant. A straight 'I can't find that out from this till,' is the best way to lose not only that customer's business but also any other they might think of bringing to you.

Attitude is important and a positive one at that.

Communication skills both verbal and written.

We looked at communication in the last chapter. In addition, there is more in *Skills for Employability Part One: Pre-Employment*.

When communicating with your customers you must put a smile in your voice if you are on the telephone or writing a memo or letter, and smile as if you are face-to-face. Grumpiness comes across in both verbal and written communication! Be positive and learn all you can about the products or work of the department. This in turn will give you confidence that you can do the job.

Part of communication is attitude and body language. Stand with chin up and shoulders back—in other words good posture. Speak clearly. If you have your chin up and shoulders back, you will be lifting your rib cage. This in turn will allow your lungs to expand as you speak and your words will come out more confidently. That is, if you pronounce your words clearly and open your mouth properly as you speak. Do not talk to your boots or mumble.

On finishing the transaction or business, smile and say good-bye and don't forget to say thank you. Ask if there is anything else the customer needs. In some situations, this can lead to another sale—especially in retail.

How to address customers.

How you address your customers will vary according to the organisation and the job role you have. If you are in a factory or workshop and a visitor comes round, a pleasant 'Good Morning' is usually enough—using the person's name if you know it.

If you are on the end of a telephone, you should at least say, 'Good Morning', followed by the name of the organisation. Tell them who is speaking. Then follow by, 'How can I help you?' *Not* a mumbled or gabbled greeting that no one can understand. Some organisations have a set way of answering the telephone. This is to make sure that everyone gives a positive impression of the organisation and maintains standards.

Written communication is usually more formal. You should address people as Mr/Mrs/Miss/Ms/Dr etc. as the case may be and end with 'Yours Sincerely' followed by your name typed and position but with a space for you to sign your name above your typed name.

The main point is to not be over-familiar but maintain friendliness and pleasantness. Again, if in doubt—ask.

Interpersonal skills.
Your personal presentation is important too as, if you are dressed cleanly and neatly you will feel better. Many organisations have some sort of company dress. This may be a top and trousers. If you are in a dirty job, you should have overalls. Even these may have the company logo on. As we said, you are the face of the organisation and your customer's expectations must not be let down. You never know to whom you are talking. That man in a battered van may actually be the boss of a company your organisation is trying to do business with!

Knowing your product or the limits of your authority will not only give you confidence but also allow you to interact with your customers in a pleasant and friendly manner.

Remember what you learned in Chapter One about equal opportunities and discrimination. You may have to grit your teeth sometimes but it is imperative that you treat everyone in the same courteous and professional manner, regardless of your personal feelings.

How to deal with minor problems.

With a willingness to please and do the job well, it is tempting to think that you can solve every problem on your own. But, beware! There are procedures to follow and, more importantly, your organisation has to follow certain legislation and regulations that apply to their particular industry.

This means that, although you want to achieve customer satisfaction, you can't always give the customer exactly what they want. It *is* important that the customer goes away happy and you *do* want them to come back again and again and bring others to buy from you.

However, when solving problems within your scope of authority, there are a few things to take into consideration.

Think about the word **HEAT**.

Do we mean it is hot? Like the weather.

Do we mean angry? You can feel the heat rising in yourself.

Do we mean a fire? A fire throws out a lot of heat.

Well yes, in a way we do, but it is more than that.

There is a way of defusing a situation by following a few simple steps. We call it:

Taking the HEAT.

Let us take these words one-by-one.

HEAR.

That means listen to the customer with your full attention. Look interested and above all do not carry on doing something else. This will infuriate your customer! Let your customer get things off their chest. They have a problem, have paid good money for something, have been inconvenienced, and had to come back to you with a complaint or problem.

EMPATHISE.

Take note—I said Em**path**ise not Em**phas**ise.

What is the difference? In the second word, *emphasise*, we mean to stress something such as a words or in speech.

In the first word, *empathise*, we mean 'be understanding of' that is, try to understand their feelings and be sympathetic.

So while you are listening to the problem take it all on board. Let the customer expel the **HEAT** and show that you are taking that HEAT. Show your concern.

APOLOGISE.

This does not mean that you are accepting responsibility or agreeing that your organisation is at fault. A simple 'I am sorry that you have a problem/ things are not right etc' takes the heat out of the situation and immediately calms the customer down, when they see that you are not going on the defensive or being negative.

TAKE OWNERSHIP.

When you are very busy and not particularly on a dedicated customer service desk it is tempting to brush the situation under the carpet, take a few notes and then forget about it. You must however, deal with the problem and if you cannot solve it yourself, go to someone who can.

Take some details. Take the customers, name, address, or telephone number as applicable, date of the transaction, or non-delivery, receipt/invoice number for tracing the order/purchase, and details of the complaint.

Some organisations have a book for customer problems. This may be the case if you are working in a retail or supplies department where deliveries are organised and arranged. If you are in an electrical retailer, there may be a problem with the product and you need to arrange for someone to come out.

Usually, they have a special book or computerised system for recording the problem/complaint. It is important that you complete this. In this way, the problem can be traced.

If you are speaking to the customer on the telephone and have to put them on hold while you speak to someone else, ask if they mind being put on hold, or would they like you to ring them back. Their time is a precious as yours. They may of course prefer to hold on.

It may be that you have to ring someone, can't get an answer, and, to save the customer waiting, suggest that you will ring them later with the outcome.

Make sure that you do so!
Some things that will help you to achieve customer satisfaction:

Follow through the problem. If you are going off shift and have left someone else to follow this up, check that it has been done. Sometimes, they slip the net.

If you are working in retail, there are usually specific procedures for dealing with returns and complaints. Follow them and make sure that you get authorisation for anything out of the ordinary which you can't deal with or that you are not sure about; in time, you will become more confident.

If you are in a stock/supplies office, you may be faced with non-deliveries. You really do have to follow this through.

Product knowledge. Know what your organisation can offer. In this way, you could suggest a suitable replacement in the case of an out of stock item and save custom. At least have the catalogues to hand for reference.

Gather all your information. Don't go back to the customer with only half a story. You are showing up yourself as incompetent and therefore the organisation.

Good communication. Looking at the above, this speaks for itself. However, whether the communication is verbal or written, you must remain professional at all times and make sure that the information is accurate and complete.

Systems and procedures. You of course have no control over these. You may be in a position, because of a problem, to suggest an improvement. The main thing now is to make sure that you know what they are—and follow them.

The important thing it to make sure that the customer experience is as perfect as you can make it and retain customer loyalty. In making the experience as perfect as you can, you will need to 'go the extra mile'. In other words, exceed customer expectations—leave them with a smile on their face and their confidence in your organisation restored and intact.

If a customer knew what 100% was, they would expect 100% every time.

Taking the **HEAT** is a way of defusing a customer and moving on to finding a solution. There is another series of problem solving steps, which you need to build in, to taking the **HEAT**.

It is the **PANDA** effect. Yes, I know, you are thinking of those huge panda's with their big soulful eyes.

The **PANDA** problem solving discipline is a five-point series of steps that covers:

```
PREPARE
  ACT
NAVIGATE
  DO
       ASSESS
```

PREPARE. Find out what has caused the problem—make notes. Check back with the customer that you have the facts right.

ACT. How are you going to solve the problem? What solutions are there?

NAVIGATE. Work out how you will implement the solution to the problem. Will a new delivery date satisfy? Will an exchange be acceptable? You want a win-win solution but not at the expense of the organisation.

DO. Carry out the solution.

ASSESS. Establish the effect of the outcome. Was the customer happy? Or was the customer putting up with the solution?

If you are lucky, your organisation will have good procedures in place for dealing with problems and complaints. At all times be pro-active and above all, do not put the customer in the wrong! The customer is king and your job relies on customer satisfaction.

Some organisations are subject to regulatory bodies, which are a last port of call if a complaint cannot be resolved. Look at your telephone bill or utility bill and you will see something in the small print about this.

Task

I want you now to think of a problem that you have either dealt with as part of a job, or led to a complaint, which you have made.

Problem One.
What was the problem?

What was the reason?

What caused the problem?

How was the problem resolved?

Was the customer /were you happy?

If not- why not?

On a scale of 1-5 with five being the best, how would you rate this experience?

If it is a problem which *you* dealt with, what was the customer's perception of your organisation?

If it is a complaint/problem, which you made/had, what was your perception of the organisation?

Re-cap.
In this chapter your have learned some of the skills needed in dealing with customers.

> ➤ Product knowledge. Knowing what your organisation produces, sells, provides.

> ➤ Communication skills—both verbal and written.

> ➤ How to address customers.

> ➤ Interpersonal skills i.e. how to interact with customers. Taking the **HEAT** and the **PANDA** effect.

You should now have more confidence in dealing with your customers both in normal situations and in dealing with problems and complaints.

Go to the next page and check your knowledge.

Check Your Knowledge.

Put the answer below without looking back on the chapter.

1. Why is it important to listen to the customer who has a problem or complaint?

2. Why is good communication essential in dealing with customers?

3. What is a customer?

4. Someone in another department in your organisation needs something doing or some information. What type of customer are they?

5. List two skills needed when dealing with a customer.

Now you can go back and check your knowledge.

Signposting to QCF.

Relationship of this chapter to the knowledge and understanding of other qualifications.

SSA 14.1 Foundations for Learning and Life.

14.2 Preparation for Work.

City & Guilds Awards and Certificates in Employability and Personal Development 7546.

> ➤ Effective skills, qualities, and attitudes for learning and work.

> ➤ Supporting others. Contributing to a team.

> ➤ Developing own interpersonal skills.

> ➤ Developing personal confidence and self-awareness.

> ➤ Dealing with challenges.

> ➤ Valuing customers.

> ➤ Solving work-related problems.

OCR Personal Life Skills.

> ➤ Forming relationships and understanding others.

OCR Employability Skills.

> ➤ Learning about workplace values and practices.

> ➤ Preparing for and learning from a work environment.

Functional Skills. English.

> ➤ Speaking, listening and communication.

> ➤ Reading

Essential Skills Wales. Communication.

> ➤ Taking part in a discussion.

> ➤ Reading.

Chapter Five. Healthy Living

In this chapter, I just want to touch on a few things, which have an effect on how you perform at work.

'Healthy living' covers a wide area. There is a wealth of information in books and magazines, which you can find at your local library, on the Internet and in your local booksellers.

Here I just want to focus on the main aspects of healthy living such as eating well, exercise, and looking after yourself.

A Google search brought up a number of websites including, http://www.nhs.uk/LiveWell/Goodfood/Pages/Goodfoodho me.aspx

Diet.

We are not talking here about going on a diet. We are talking about making sure that the foods you eat—your diet—contains all the nutrients needed to maintain a healthy body.

The human body needs a mix of foods to stay healthy; in other words a balanced diet. There are different food groups.

We all need vitamins and minerals. These are found in fruit and vegetables.

Some vitamins are fat-soluble and some are water-soluble.

Fat-soluble vitamins are Vitamins A, D, E, and K. They are found mainly in foods such as butter, lard, oily fish, and dairy foods to name a few. If you have more of these than you need, the surplus is stored in the liver and fatty tissues of your body ready for when your body does need them. Therefore, you do not need to eat them every day even though your body needs them every day to work properly.

Having too much more than you need could be harmful. It is all about balance.

Water-soluble vitamins are not stored in the body. Any surplus of these vitamins is simply discharged from the body when you go to the toilet. As they are not stored, you need to have them every day. Water-soluble vitamins are found in fruit vegetables and grain. They can be destroyed by heat, being exposed to the air, or be lost in water during cooking. Therefore, it is important to store fruit and vegetables properly and not to overcook them. Otherwise, all the nutrients are lost. Water-soluble vitamins are Vitamins C, the B vitamin family, and folic acid.

Minerals build strong bones and teeth, control body fluids, and convert food into energy. Meat, cereals and cereal products, milk, fish, dairy products, vegetables, fruit, and nuts all contain minerals. The essentials minerals, which our body needs, are calcium and iron.

Trace elements such as fluoride and iodine are something else, which our body needs to function properly and stay healthy. They are found in small amounts in foods such as meat, fish, cereals, dairy foods, nuts, and vegetables.

Carbohydrates are another essential part of a balanced diet. We all need carbohydrates. These are found in starchy foods such as bread and pasta potatoes, cereals, rice. They give us energy.

(Have you noticed that the same foods keep appearing?)

Fat. You will have heard a lot about fat and how to avoid it. We do however need a certain amount of fat. But we need the good fats.
Taking too much saturated fat can lead to raised cholesterol in the blood, giving rise to a risk of heart disease. So all the things we like such as hard cheese, cakes, biscuits, sausages, cream, for example are bad for us if we have too much. Cakes, biscuits, and fizzy drinks also have a lot of added

sugars, which are not good for us. On the other hand, the natural sugars found in fruit and milk are a better option.

Unsaturated fats are healthier and are found in vegetable oils, avocados, and oily fish. Try cutting off the fat from cuts of meat.

Salt. The cereals, breads, and sauces we buy also contain salt and too much is bad for us. When cooking, try not adding salt to the pan but leave it to the person eating to decide if they need a touch to suit their palate.

Protein. Protein is essential for the body to function properly. It is needed for healthy hair and fingernails, for growth and so that it can repair itself. Protein is found in meat, poultry, eggs, shellfish, soya products, pulses, nuts, and seeds for example.

You will by now, be getting the picture. http://www.bbc.co.uk/health/treatments/healthy_living/nu trition/healthy_protein.shtml

Calories. Calories are a measurement of energy contained in the food and drink, which we consume. During exercise and movement, the body needs energy. Calories are burned to produce this energy.

If you eat and drink more than you burn off, the surplus is stored as fat. It depends on your lifestyle.

Eating less than we need means that your body draws on reserves of fat stored in the body.

Even if you are eating less than you need, you need to eat less of the foods that are high in calories and not simply *less food*, as your body still needs food in order to function properly.

The trick is to eat a balanced diet of foods that provide energy, vitamins, and minerals, together with maintaining fluids levels with water. Herbal teas are also good for you. Also, make sure that the food you eat contains enough fibre so that your body remains a regular cycle. Eat wholemeal bread, fruit, vegetables, and high fibre cereals.

Task 🖊

Make a list of which foods contain:

1. Vitamins and minerals.✓

2. Protein.✓

3. Carbohydrate✓

Salt.**X**

Saturated Fat **X**

Unsaturated Fat. ✓

Which foods appear more frequently in the 'good foods'?

Can you name others not listed here?

Exercise.

There are many ways of exercising from walking, running, going to the gym, gardening, playing tennis, and dancing, to name a few.

Exercise keeps us healthy and maintains healthy joints and muscles. It is also good for our mental health.

Sleep.

It is tempting to stay up late to watch a film or to stay out late in the pub or club. However, a good night's sleep is important for our general health. It is during sleep that our body repairs cells, re-charges its batteries, and works to keep our mind and body in tip-top condition. We can manage on less sleep for only a short period—and everyone is different in their needs. If we are deprived of enough sleep for too long, we cease to function efficiently with the result that our performance is affected. Having achieved the goal of getting the job, you want to keep it. Don't you?

The old maxim 'early to bed, early to rise, makes you healthy, wealthy and wise', is not far off the mark.

http://www.helpguide.org/life/sleeping.htm

Personal hygiene.

In an earlier chapter in this book and in *Skills for Employability Part One: Pre-Employment,* we talked about personal presentation at work.

One aspect of this is the more delicate topic of personal hygiene. You may think that it doesn't matter but other people have to work alongside you.

You might think that your socks are not dirty. Well, *you* think that they don't smell. Just because you can't smell them doesn't mean that they don't. It depends on your sense of smell. If you have a real problem with smelly feet, or foot odour to give it its correct name, there are products on the market to deal with this. Sometimes the foods you eat are the cause. Changing your shoes helps as they have a chance to dry out. Don't wear the same pair two days running.

If you perspire a lot, you will possibly find large patches of sweat under your armpits. There is a natural smell to all of us. It only becomes a problem of body odour or B.O. when washing and showering routines are neglected.

You may find that you need to shower/bathe both morning and night. If you are in a dirty job—one that leaves you feeling grubby—or you are going out, you most likely will want a shower when you get home from work. A good hot shower followed by a nice tangy aftershave or perfume is a great pick-me-up.

The benefits of a shower or bath in the morning are not to be underestimated. It will wake you up and leave you feeling ready to greet the challenges of the day. Don't forget a deodorant for your underarms and a special one or talc for your feet if needed.

Clean clothes are essential. At the very least a clean shirt/blouse and socks/tights every day are a must in keeping fresh. Outer garments and nightwear should be changed on a regular basis. If clothes are not washable, then they must be dry-cleaned. With the technological developments in fabrics, many garments, which at one time had to be dry-cleaned, are now washable.

Clean your teeth with nice fresh toothpaste. There are also many flossing products on the market to remove the debris from hard to reach places between your teeth. It helps to prevent plaque forming which will be one less job for the dentist.

Regular dental appointments are essential in maintaining dental hygiene.

Re-cap.

In this chapter, we have touched on some aspects of healthy living. Food, diet, eating well, exercise, and personal hygiene. There are many other aspects to healthy living. Follow the links in this chapter and see where they lead you.

Good luck with the job and don't forget! Dress to impress! Look up to where you are going!

Check Your Knowledge.

Put your answers below without looking back on the chapter.

1. List four products needed for personal hygiene.

a)

b)

c)

d)

2. Why is it important to shower/bathe at least once every day?

Which vitamins are fat-soluble?

What are the benefits of exercise?

Now go back and check your knowledge

Signposting to QCF.

Relationship of this chapter to the knowledge and understanding of other qualifications.

SSA 14.1 Foundations for Learning and Life.

14.2 Preparation for Work.

City & Guilds Awards and Certificates in Employability and Personal Development 7546.

> ➤ Effective skills, qualities, and attitudes for learning and work.

> ➤ Healthy living.

> ➤ Personal body hygiene awareness.

> ➤ Introduction to general health and hygiene skills.

> ➤ Developing skills for a healthy lifestyle.

> ➤ Developing skills for hygiene and health.

> ➤ Healthy eating in personal development.

> ➤ Personal presentation in the workplace.

OCR Personal Life Skills.

> ➤ Introducing personal health and wellbeing.

> ➤ Understanding how to maintain personal health and wellbeing.

> ➤ Maintaining and improving health and wellbeing.

Progression. Where do I go from here?

After reading and completing *Skills for Employability Part Two: Moving into Employment,* you may want to buy *Skills for Employability Part One: Pre-Employment* if you haven't already done so. Just to re-cap on some of the topics and have the complete picture. It is in the same non-threatening, user-friendly format, with space to complete a few tasks.

Depending on 'where you are at' in the scheme of things, you may be ready to think a little more about what you want to do and what your goals are. When you left school, you most likely would have been given a Record of Achievement folder with evidence of your courses and exams. It doesn't end here. You must keep up a record of what you have done both in work and in private life. Remember! No learning is ever wasted so record it all—formal, and informal through activities.

Many employers now are asking for some evidence that you have taken control of your learning and development, not only for your future success but also for that of the organisation. *Release Your Potential: Making Sense of Personal and Professional Development* takes the mystery out of this process and helps you to focus on your goals in life.

Your employer may be in a position to offer a training programme. 'But you said earlier that I should be trained on how to do things and use equipment,' I can hear you say.

Yes, I did, but I am talking about your future in a wider sense. There are all sorts of practical short courses on various aspects of the job. Are your IT skills up to scratch? Would you benefit from working towards the European Computer

Driving Licence (ECDL) qualification. I remember when this was first developed and we were all excited that there was an IT course that would be more widely recognised. Now, you can do it on-line from various locations with a dedicated on-line tutor to support you. If you already have these skills then you could try the Advanced ECDL, which would take your skills to a higher level and enhance your future even more.

When we think of apprenticeships, we think in terms of engineering, electrical, manufacturing etc. However, apprenticeships cover all types of occupations. You are earning while you are learning. They are designed in what we call a framework. By this I mean that there is a programme which provides the essential knowledge you need in order to acquire the skills;, a competence based qualification where you have the opportunity to show that you can do the job; and Functional Skills which are the underpinning skills in Communication/English, Maths' number skills and Information and Communication Technology—which you need in life in order to function in any setting.

These programmes are work-based and a valuable way to gain skills and knowledge to prove that you are competent in your job and work towards a better future.

Contact your local Job Centre or college to find out about more training opportunities, or a new one, in your area.

Follow the links in the next section for more information.

Useful Links and Resources

http://www.apprenticeships.org.uk/Be-An-Apprentice.aspx

http://wales.gov.uk/topics/educationandskills/learningprovi
ders/essentialskillswales/

http://www.direct.gov.uk/en/Employment/Employees/inde
x.htm

http://www.direct.gov.uk/en/Employment/Employees/The
NationalMinimumWage/DG_10027201

http://www.bis.gov.uk/search?keywords=contracts+of+emp
loyment&type=all

http://www.thepensionsregulator.gov.uk/workplacepension
s.html

http://www.pcs.org.uk/en/resources/health_and_safety/he
alth_and_safety_legal_summaries/display_screen_equipm
ent_regulations.cfm

http://www.hse.gov.uk/pubns/ppeindex.htm

http://www.worksmart.org.uk/

http://www.worksmart.org.uk/rights/health_and_safety

http://www.worksmart.org.uk/rights/i_have_heard_about_
a_duty_of 07.03.2012

http://www.healthandsafety.co.uk/CHOOSING%20THE%2
0RIGHT%20CHAIR.pdf

http://www.mfs-fire-extinguishers.co.uk/types.htm

http://www.hmrc.gov.uk/rates/it.htm

http://en.wikipedia.org/wiki/Communication

http://www.ecdl.org/

http://dataprotectionact.org/1.html

http://www.ico.gov.uk/

http://www.ipo.gov.uk/c-about.htm

http://www.bbc.co.uk/schools/gcsebitesize/

http://homeoffice.gov.uk/equalities/equality-act/

http://www.cepr.org/aboutcepr/policies.htm

http://www.equalityhumanrights.com/human-rights/

http://www.bbc.co.uk/schools/gcsebitesize/business/enviro
nment/acompetitivemarketrev1.shtml

http://www.nhs.uk/LiveWell/Goodfood/Pages/Goodfoodho
me.aspx http://www.thefreedictionary.com/ethics

http://www.bbc.co.uk/health/treatments/healthy_living/nu
trition/healthy_protein.shtml

http://www.helpguide.org/life/sleeping.htm

htp://www.google.com

Chantler. J. How to Pass Customer Service, Third Level.P62
Prescott. C.R./Shoemark. S. Certificate in Customer Service
Level 2. Yale College 2005.

Morris. J. R. Health and Safety: A Guide for the Newly
Appointed. Cassell-ISM 1997 p8-10).

Further Reading

Lifelong Learning: Personal Effectiveness Guides.

Initially, the series will look at the background to lifelong learning and some research into various viewpoints.

Following this, will be an introduction on how to structure and develop your continuing personal development records. The basic principles here can be applied to any level in various degrees of complexity and are suitable for a cross-section of ages and occupations.

The series continues with the skills needed for employability and are in two parts.

Whom are these books for?
- ➢ Aimed at the home learner and designed to read in bite-sized chunks.
- ➢ Someone who is unable to attend formal courses.
- ➢ To fill gaps in underpinning knowledge and skills needed to 'get on in life'.
- ➢ Designed as a user-friendly support material for learners of all ages with a wide range of abilities.

Lifelong Learning: A View from the Coal Face.

ISBN 978-1-908302-04-5. Also in e-book formats for most e-readers.

This is the first of the new Lifelong Learning: Personal Effectiveness Guides by Rosalie Marsh, which draw from her extensive skills & industrial experience in sales management and work-based learning in adult and further education.

This springboard for this new series of Lifelong Learning: Personal Effectiveness Guides revisits earlier research carried out which examined:

- ➤ Lifelong learning.
- ➤ It's meaning.
- ➤ The governments of the day's perspective and aspirations for the future.
- ➤ The experiences of a cross-section of professionals and educators when they were at school.
- ➤ The effects of the educational policies of the day on their progress then and that of their employees.

The research is brought up-to-date with a reflection of 'where we are now' and reference to the Wolf Report. It brings a new perspective and focus to this very relevant issue today.

The author looks at the wider issues of:

- ➤ Learning.
- ➤ Opportunity.
- ➤ Access.
- ➤ Professional and Personal Development, before asking if the success of the initiatives is being effectively measured.

The results of the semi-structured interviews with a cross-section of mature adults had surprising results.

Release Your Potential: Making Sense of Personal and Professional Development.
ISBN 978-1-908302-08-3. Also in e-book formats for most e-readers.

This is the second of the new Lifelong Learning: Personal Effectiveness Guides by Rosalie Marsh, which draw from her extensive skills & industrial experience in sales management and work-based learning in adult and further education.

You are having a career change; you are looking to get into employment; you are looking to simply become more effective in your present role but don't know how to go about improving your skills.

If this sounds familiar—
Release Your Potential will help you to:

> ➢ Identify what you know now and need to know in order to improve.
> ➢ Look at how you learn best.
> ➢ Make best use of your time.
> ➢ Handle stress.
> ➢ Plan how you will achieve your goals.
> ➢ Develop and maintain a Personal Development Portfolio.

Skills for Employability.

Further titles in the new Lifelong Learning: Personal Effectiveness Guides by Rosalie Marsh, which draw from her extensive skills & industrial experience in sales management and work-based learning in adult and further education. It is a step in the personal and professional development journey where development of the whole person is at the heart of Rosalie's ethos.

In two parts, *Skills for Employability*—designed to be read in bite-sized chunks—will focus on some of the skills you need in order to impress an employer, stand out from the rest, become employed, and enhance your future.

Part One looks at the pre-employment skills needed.
ISBN 978-1-908302-16-8. Also in e-book formats for most e-readers.

Part Two looks at what you need to know when you move into employment.
ISBN 978-1-908302-20-5. Also in e-book formats for most e-readers.

Each chapter details the learning outcomes and relevance to other qualifications such as Personal Life Skills, Employability Skills, and Functional Skills. Through short practical activities, the learner will be able to see how far you have 'travelled' in gaining knowledge and understanding.

Skills for Employability Part One: Pre-Employment looks at those skills for the future, which include:

- ➤ Preparing for work.
- ➤ Job applications and a successful interview.
- ➤ Working effectively in the workplace.
- ➤ ICT skills in the workplace.

Skills for Employability Part Two: Moving into Employment looks at the standards of behaviour and requirements of employers:

> An introduction to health and safety in the workplace and Employment Rights and Responsibilities (ERR).
> The business environment and good working relationships.
> The importance of good customer service.
> Important aspects of managing your money.
> Progression. 'Where do I go from here?'

Some of the benefits of Skills for Employability.

> User-friendly. Can work at your own pace.
> Raised self-esteem and confidence.
> An increased awareness of the standards of behaviour and requirements of employers.
> An awareness and understanding of the business environment.

Whom are these books for?

> School leavers; 16-18 yr old unemployed; returners to work; learners seeking a change of employment, wishing to enhance their prospects or, are between jobs.
> Aimed at the home learner and someone who is unable to attend formal courses.
> To fill gaps in underpinning knowledge and skills needed to 'get on in life'.

Just Us Two Travel Series.
During their first Gold Wing experience, finding that the words flowed when recounting their profound emotional experiences, Rosalie realised that there was the beginnings of a story. As the years passed, they extended their horizons, travelling over 50,000 miles on their own. Rosalie wrote about their amazing experiences as feature articles, eventually concluding that together they formed an inspiring story of adventure and realisation of dreams. Rosalie wanted to share their story and so, with the support of 'Ned', *her* baby was born.

Just Us Two: Ned and Rosie's Gold Wing Discovery.
ISBN 978-1-908302-12-0. Also in e-book formats for most e-readers.
Winner 2010 International Book Awards (Travel: Recreational).
Finalist 2009 Best Books Awards (Travel: Recreational). USA Book News.

Just Us Two is an exhilarating romp through ten happy years of discovery, adventure, and fun! Ned, in middle age wanted a little bike to tinker with. Rosie discovered a majestic Gold Wing motorbike and swopped well-groomed hair and high heels for a crash helmet and biker's boots. Share their thrills and spills as they discover long lost family in Ireland before jaunting around Europe to follow Rosie's dreams... travelling on their own—*Just Us Two.*

What readers say about Just Us Two.

'Inspiration for us all to motorcycle touring overseas.'
Editor Motorbike Search Engine.
http://motorbike-search-engine.co.uk/motorcycle-product-reviews.php.

'Not just for bikers!'
'Rosalie's passion for travel, adventure, and living life to the full comes across so beautifully in her narrative and her book Just Us Two, which I highly recommend. Rosalie's thirst for knowledge and personal development has driven her to write and share her wonderful experiences – a true inspiration to me and I believe to anyone who aspires to live life without 'if onlys'.
Chrisoula Sirigou, ExploramaEU.

'The descriptions . . . so wonderful I felt I was there, on the motorbike.'
Jean Mead. Author.

'A gifted author who can bring her travels books alive. She has a wonderful sense of the ridiculous and her style as a raconteur means that the reader feels she is talking personally.'
Judith Sharman. Well-Tree-Learning.

'A great read that will make you smile.'
Editor, Trike Magazine.

Read the sequel *Chasing Rainbows: with Just Us Two.* The second in the Just Us Two series and the real ending to Rosie's Gold Wing story.

Chasing Rainbows: with Just Us Two.

ISBN 978-1-908302-00-7. Also in e-book formats for most e-readers.

Sat Navs! Do you love them or hate them?

Chasing Rainbows is the real ending to Rosie's Gold Wing story. Now, no longer able to ride, this intrepid couple finally say good-bye their Gold Wing motorbiking days but only after more adventures; this time not on a Honda Gold Wing'; this time not quite Just Us Two . . .

In this new saga, a hidden controller, in the shape of disembodied voice with which Rosie conducts a 'love-hate' relationship as it threatened to make her navigating skills redundant and ruin their next big trip, accompanies them.

Now, 'Ned' has come out of the shadows and reverted to his given name, which is how he appears in this light-hearted and often tongue in cheek story of discovery and adventures. He also has a new toy. You know boys and their toys. It is infallible; trusty will lead them to wherever they want to go. No stress; no trouble; no getting lost . . .

Take in the beauty of Ireland and Co.Mayo; the breathtaking wonder of the Andorran mountains; the awesome grandeur of the Spanish Pyrenees; Visit Versailles and Paris as Rosie chases her rainbows . . .

What readers say about Chasing Rainbows.

'Another great book by Rosalie Marsh that should not be missed. The flow of words employed to narrate it, is in itself most refreshing.' Joseph Abela, Author, on Chasing Rainbows.

'A great follow up to Just Us Two.' Amazon reader, on Chasing Rainbows.

Rosalie Marsh titles are available worldwide in print and e-book formats for most readers.

Christal Publishing

www.christalpublishing.com

CPSIA information can be obtained at www.ICGtesting.com
Printed in the USA
LVOW011551211212

312799LV00016B/535/P